COMPANIONS FOR THE JOURNEY

Praying with
Teresa of Ávila

Rosemary Broughton

theWORD
among us®
press

Published by The Word Among Us Press
9639 Doctor Perry Road
Ijamsville, Maryland 21754
www.wordamongus.org

12 11 10 09 08   1 2 3 4 5
ISBN: 978-0-932085-88-7

Cover design: The DesignWorks Group
Cover Image: Peter Paul Rubens,
Heilige Therese von Avila, 1615
Museum of Art History, Vienna, Austria

Acknowledgments begin on p. 141.

Made and printed in the United States of America

Library of Congress Control Number: 2008921220

Contents

Foreword

J ust as food is required for human life, so are companions. Indeed, the word "companions" comes from two Latin words: *com,* meaning "with," and *panis,* meaning "bread." Companions nourish our heart, mind, soul, and body. They are also the people with whom we can celebrate the sharing of bread.

Perhaps the most touching stories in the Bible are about companionship: the Last Supper, the wedding feast at Cana, the sharing of the loaves and the fishes, and Jesus' breaking bread with the disciples on the road to Emmaus. Each incident of companionship with Jesus revealed more about his mercy, love, wisdom, suffering, and hope. When Jesus went to pray in the Garden of Olives, he craved the companionship of the apostles. They let him down. But God sent the Spirit to inflame the hearts of the apostles, and they became faithful companions to Jesus and to each other.

Throughout history, other faithful companions have followed Jesus and the apostles. These saints and mystics have also taken the journey from conversion, through suffering, to resurrection. Just as they were inspired by the holy people who went before them, so too may you take them as your companions as you walk on your spiritual journey.

The Companions for the Journey series is a response to the spiritual hunger of Christians. This series makes available the rich spiritual teachings of mystics and guides whose wisdom can help us on our pilgrimage. Our hope is that, as you complete each meditation, you will feel supported, challenged, and affirmed by a soul-companion on your spiritual journey.

The spiritual hunger that has emerged in the last few decades is a great sign of renewal in Christian life. People fill retreat programs and workshops on topics about spirituality. The demand for spiritual directors exceeds the number available. Interest in the lives and writings of saints and mystics is increasing as people search for models of whole and holy Christian life.

PRAYING WITH THE SAINTS

Praying with Teresa of Ávila is more than just a book about Teresa's spirituality. This book seeks to engage you in praying in the way that Teresa of Ávila did about issues and themes that were central to her experience. Each meditation can enlighten your understanding of her revelations and lead you to reflect on your own experience.

The goal of *Praying with Teresa of Ávila* is that you will discover her wonderfully alive spirituality and integrate her spirit and wisdom into your relationship with God, with your brothers and sisters, and with your own heart and mind.

Suggestions for Praying with Teresa of Ávila

Meet Teresa of Ávila, a caring companion for your pilgrimage, by reading the Introduction, which begins on page 13. It provides a brief biography and the major themes of her spirituality.

Once you meet Teresa of Ávila, you will be ready to pray with her and to encounter God, your human sisters and brothers, and yourself in new and wonderful ways. To help your prayer, here are some suggestions that have been part of the tradition of Christian spirituality:

Create a sacred space. Jesus said, "Whenever you pray, go into your room and shut the door and pray to your Father who is in secret; and your Father who sees in secret will reward you" (Matthew 6:6). Solitary prayer is best done in a place where you can have privacy and silence, both of which can be luxuries in the lives of busy people. If privacy and silence are not possible, create a quiet, safe place within yourself, perhaps while riding to and from work, while waiting in the dentist's office, or while waiting for someone. Do the best you can, knowing that a loving God is present everywhere. Whether the meditations in this book are used for solitary prayer or with a group, try to create a prayerful mood with candles, meditative music, a crucifix, or an image of Mary.

Open yourself to the power of prayer. Every human experience has a religious dimension. All of life is suffused with God's presence. So remind yourself that God is present as you begin your period of prayer. Do not worry about distractions. If something keeps intruding during your prayer, spend some time talking with God about it. Be flexible, because God's Spirit blows where it will.

Prayer can open your mind and widen your vision. Be open to new ways of seeing God, people, and yourself. As you open yourself to the Spirit of God, different emotions are evoked, such as sadness from tender memories, or joy from a celebration recalled. Our emotions are messages from God that can tell us much about our spiritual quest. Also, prayer strengthens our will to act. Through prayer, God can touch our will and empower us to live according to what we know is true.

Finally, many of the meditations in this book will call you to employ your memories, your imagination, and the circumstances of your life as subjects for prayer. The great mystics and saints realized that they had to use all of their resources to know God better. Indeed, God speaks to us continually and touches us constantly. We must learn to listen and feel with all the means that God gave us.

Come to prayer with an open mind, heart, and will.

Preview each meditation before beginning. Spend a few moments previewing the readings and especially the reflection activities. Several reflection activities are given in each meditation, because different styles of prayer appeal to different personalities or personal needs. *Note that each meditation has more reflection activities than can be done during one prayer period. Therefore, select only one or two reflection activities each time you use a meditation. Do not feel compelled to complete all of the reflection activities.*

Read meditatively. After you have placed yourself in God's presence, the meditations offer you a story about Teresa and a selection from her writings. Take your time reading. If a particular phrase touches you, stay with it. Relish its feelings, meanings, and concerns.

Use the reflections. Following "Teresa's Words" is a short reflection in commentary form, meant to give perspective to the readings. Then you will be offered several ways of meditating on the readings and the theme of the prayer. You may be familiar with the different methods of meditating, but in case you are not, they are described briefly here:

≈ Repeated centering prayer: One means of focusing your prayer is to use a centering prayer. The prayer may be a single word or a short phrase taken from the readings or from the Scriptures. For example, a centering prayer for a meditation on courage might be "I go before you" or "trust." Repeated slowly in harmony with your breathing, the prayer helps you center your heart and mind on one action or attribute of God.

🍃 *Lectio divina:* This type of meditation is "divine studying," a concentrated reflection on the word of God or the wisdom of a spiritual writer. Most often in *lectio divina,* you will be invited to read one of the passages several times and then concentrate on one or two sentences, pondering their meaning for you and their effect on you. *Lectio divina* commonly ends with formulation of a resolution.

🍃 Guided meditation: In this type of meditation, our imagination helps us consider alternative actions and likely consequences. Our imagination helps us experience new ways of seeing God, our neighbors, ourselves, and nature. When Jesus told his followers parables and stories, he engaged their imagination. In this book you will be asked to follow a guided meditation.

One way of doing a guided meditation is to read the scene or story several times until you know the outline and can recall it when you enter into reflection. Or, before your prayer time, you may wish to record the meditation on a tape recorder. If so, remember to allow pauses for reflection between phrases and to speak with a slow, peaceful pace and tone. Then, during prayer, when you have finished the readings and the reflection commentary, you can turn on your recording of the meditation and be led through it. If you find your own voice too distracting, ask a friend to make the tape for you.

❧ Examen of consciousness: The reflections often will ask you to examine how God has been speaking to you in your past and present experience—in other words, the reflections will ask you to examine your awareness of God's presence in your life.

❧ Journal writing: Writing is a process of discovery. If you write for any length of time, stating honestly what is on your mind and in your heart, you will unearth much about who you are, how you stand with your God, what deep longings reside in your soul, and more. In some of the reflections, you may be asked to write a dialogue with Jesus or someone else. If you have never used writing as a means of meditation, try it. Reserve a special notebook for your journal writing. If desired, you can go back to your entries at a future time for an examen of consciousness.

❧ Action: Occasionally, a reflection may suggest singing a favorite hymn, going out for a walk, or undertaking some other physical activity. Actions can be meaningful forms of prayer.

Using the Meditations for Group or Family Prayer

If you wish to use the meditations for community prayer, these suggestions may be of help:

🙰 Read the theme to the group. Call the group into the presence of God, using the short opening prayer. Invite one or two participants to read one or both of the readings. If you use both readings, observe the pause between them.

🙰 You may decide to use the reflection as a reading or to skip it, depending on the needs and interests of the group.

🙰 Select one of the reflection activities for your group. Allow sufficient time for your group to reflect, to do a centering prayer, to accomplish a studying prayer (*lectio divina*), or to finish an examen of consciousness. Depending on the group and the amount of time available, you may want to invite the participants to share their reflections, responses, or petitions with the group.

🙰 Reading the passage from the Scriptures may serve as a summary of the meditation.

🙰 If a formulated prayer or a psalm is given as a closing, it may be recited by the entire group. Or you may ask participants to offer their own prayers for the closing.

Now you are ready to pray with Teresa of Ávila, a compassionate and challenging companion on your spiritual journey. May you find her to be a true companion for your soul.

Introduction:
The Attraction of Teresa

Teresa of Ávila is a woman, a saint, a mystic, and a doctor of the church. She is best known for her reform of the Carmelite community in sixteenth-century Spain and for her many inspiring and profound writings that were saved and circulated in the decades after her death. As a woman of prayer, Teresa is a good model for anyone who wants to live a simple life with God in the midst of a complex world.

Teresa was a favorite of Dorothy Day, one of the founders of the Catholic Worker Movement. In *The Long Loneliness*, Dorothy Day tells why she named her daughter Tamar Teresa:

I had read the life of St. Teresa of Ávila and fallen in love with her. She was a mystic and a practical woman, a recluse and a traveler, a cloistered nun and yet most active. She liked to read novels when she was a young girl, and she wore a bright red dress when she entered the convent. Once when she was traveling from one part of Spain to another with some other nuns and a priest to start a convent, and their way took them over a stream, she was thrown from her donkey. The story goes that our Lord said to her, "That is how I treat my friends." And she replied, "And that is why You have so few of them."

She called life a "night spent at an uncomfortable inn." Once when she was trying to avoid that recreation hour which is set aside in convents for nuns to be together, the others insisted on her joining them, and she took castanets and danced. When some older nuns professed themselves shocked, she retorted, "One must do things sometimes to make life more bearable." . . . And there were other delightful little touches to the story of her life which made me love her and feel close to her. (pp. 140–141)

Dorothy Day's comments hint at why Teresa of Ávila has remained popular with Christians. But is Teresa a good companion for *your* journey?

She is, if you enjoy solitude and do not know why. Teresa frequently expresses in her writings what we may be experiencing in the depths of our souls.

She is, if you are attracted to a spirit of adventure in life and in your relationship with God. Teresa was a woman who took risks but had a head full of common sense.

She is, if you discern a deeper call to prayer and to intimacy with Christ in your life. In her writings, Teresa describes stages that are normal—but that are sometimes experienced as paradoxical—in growing in union with God.

She is, if you find yourself confronting cultural complexities while trying to bring about reform. Teresa modeled patient determination and a basic confidence that God is with us, working in this world.

Teresa's Story

Teresa lived during one of the most dynamic periods in Spanish history. Spain was exploring and conquering the New World. The achievements of Spanish artists and scientists were setting new standards. And the spirit of reform was beginning to spread into the Spanish church.

Early Life

Teresa was born on March 28, 1515, in Ávila, Spain. She was the first daughter of Doña Beatriz de Ahumada, who had already borne two sons. Teresa also had an older brother and sister from her father's first marriage. Eventually, there were twelve children in her family. Teresa's father, Don Alonso Sánchez de Cepeda, was a cloth merchant, a profession he inherited from his father, who was a Jewish-Christian.

Teresa said little about her childhood. But she did say that her parents modeled, in their gracious care of their children, both personal piety and social compassion.

One story Teresa did tell explains the context of her initial devotion to God. Evidently, Teresa and her favorite brother avidly read about the lives of the saints. Teresa once said, "When I considered the martyrdoms the saints suffered for God, it seemed to me that the price they paid for going to enjoy God was very cheap, and I greatly desired to die in the same way." Teresa and her brother decided to be martyrs so that they could rapidly attain the joys of heaven. After long deliberations, the two children settled on heading to "the land of the Moors," where they figured they would get their heads cut off. Once they had planned their journey, Teresa and her brother realized that they had a major problem: "Having parents seemed to us the greatest obstacle" (*The Book of Her Life*, in *The Collected Works of of St. Teresa Ávila*, vol. 1, trans. Kavanaugh and Rodriguez, p. 55).

Since they could not be martyred, Teresa and her loyal brother plotted to be hermits. Indeed, the two tried to build a little hermitage from piled-up stones that kept collapsing. Teresa gave alms to others, even though she had little to give. With her girl companions, Teresa pretended to be a nun living in community, although she preferred being a martyr or at least a hermit over being a nun. These motifs of martyr and hermit, almsgiver and companion, came to permeate Teresa's adult life.

Adolescence

Surrounded by her siblings and cousins in a close family, Teresa seemed to have led a happy childhood. Then, in 1528, her mother died. Later, Teresa wrote, "When I began to understand what I had lost, I went, afflicted, before an image of our Lady and besought her with many tears to be my mother. It seems to me that although I did this in simplicity it helped me" (*Life*, p. 56).

As an adolescent, Teresa became absorbed in the typical concerns of that age group. She spent much time—which she later judged as frivolous—with cousins close to her own age. Teresa desired a good social image and reputation. The cultural norms of honor both preserved and tempted her and, by her own acknowledgment, she sometimes put on a false front. One story tells of Teresa attending a ball shortly before she entered the Carmelites. A young man evidently admired her pretty feet in their dancing slippers. Teresa supposedly quipped, "Take a good look, sir. You won't be getting another chance" (Phyllis McGinley, *Saint-Watching*, p. 93).

In 1531, Teresa's father sent her to the Augustinians' convent school of Our Lady of Grace, but the next year she left because of high fevers and fainting spells. She convalesced for a time at her uncle's home in Hortigosa and later at her older sister's home in Castellanos de la Cañada. Love and care nurtured Teresa in both places. This period of illness also gave her time to reflect on the meaning of life and her own religious beliefs.

When Teresa returned to her father's home, she continued to read religious books. Gradually, she decided to become a Carmelite. One factor in her decision to join the Carmelites was that her good friend, Juana Suárez, had entered this community. However, Teresa's father would not consent to her leaving home, so she left secretly. At twenty years of age, she entered the Carmelite Monastery of the Incarnation.

Life in the Incarnation Monastery

The Carmelite community finds its origins in legends of a group of hermits located at Mount Carmel, northeast of Galilee where Jesus lived. These hermits were dedicated to Mary, whom they claimed lived her childhood at Mount Carmel. They also continued a long tradition of prophetic men, such as Elijah and Eliseus, who came to the desert to be healed, consoled, and challenged by prayer. In the twelfth or thirteenth century, these monks went to the West and began founding communities.

According to the accepted tradition in Teresa's time, in the thirteenth century Albert of Jerusalem had written a rule for the monks that was later called the "primitive rule." According to Teresa, this rule explained the contemplative ideals:

First, to offer God a heart holy and pure of all stain of actual sin (through one's own efforts assisted by grace); second, to taste at times, by divine gift, God's sweetness in the depths of one's heart and to experience in one's soul the power of His divine presence. (Kieran Kavanaugh, *The Book of Her Foundations—Introduction*, in *The Collected Works of St. Teresa of Ávila*, vol. 3, p. 16)

Periodically in the following centuries, the rule was adapted and modified. By the sixteenth century, Carmelites lived under what was called the "mitigated rule."

Early Years as a Carmelite

In the fifteenth century, Carmelite monasteries for women were established. The Monastery of Incarnation was one of the eleven Carmelite communities in Spain in the sixteenth century. It housed approximately one hundred and fifty nuns. The Incarnation Monastery depended on endowments from wealthy people. The cultivation of benefactors and continuation of good relations with them demanded much time and energy.

According to the customs of the period, the women entering the monastery—especially if they came with a substantial dowry—lived in a suite of rooms and could keep servants, relatives, or friends with them. If sisters became seriously ill and food supplies were low, they became dependent on relatives and friends, sometimes living with them for a period of recovery.

The sisters kept rules of silence and fasted during the seasons when the food supply was not plentiful. With song and ceremony, they recited the Divine Office together. The sisters both received and gave spiritual counsel, and they ministered to sick people and those recently bereaved if a request was made to the superior.

In the initial fervor of her vocation, Teresa feared imperfection. She became upset over unimportant situations and bore the hurt of accusations about things that were not her fault: "I was fond of everything about religious life, but I didn't like to suffer anything that seemed to be scorn. I enjoyed being esteemed. I was meticulous about everything I did" (*Life*, p. 70).

Nevertheless, Teresa acknowledged early on that life at the Incarnation did not follow the rule required for deep prayer and contemplation. "The convent," she said, "was not founded on a strict observance. I, miserable creature that I was, followed after what I saw wrong and left aside the good" (*Life*, p. 70). The sisters' mitigated observance of the Carmelite rule made it difficult for them to find uninterrupted time for silence, prayer, and meditation. Friends and relatives came rather freely to visit the sisters.

Years of Illness

From 1538 to 1542, serious illnesses struck Teresa and brought her close to death's door.

During this time, Teresa moved from the Convent of the Incarnation to her family's home. However, she eventually returned to the convent. Later, Teresa described one of her bouts of illness:

Such were these four days I spent in this paroxysm that only the Lord can know the unbearable torments I suffered within myself: my tongue, bitten to pieces; my throat unable to let even water pass down—from not having swallowed anything and from great weakness that oppressed me; everything seeming to be disjointed; the greatest confusion in my head; all shriveled and drawn together in a ball. The result of the torments of those four days was that I unable to stir, not an arm or a foot, neither hand nor head, unable to move as though I were dead; only one finger on my right hand it seems I was able to move. Since there was no way of touching me, because I was so bruised that I couldn't endure it, they moved me about in a sheet, one of the nuns at one end and another at the other. (*Life*, p. 76)

Teresa's agony continued for a long time after these initial days. Her paralysis lasted almost three years. Eventually, she dragged herself around on her hands and knees. After the fourth year, Teresa returned to a measure of health, although various ailments continued to plague her.

Inner Division and Conversion
Teresa described her religious life at the Incarnation as a contradiction to the things that she found when she turned to God in prayer. She amused herself with various pastimes. She grew "ashamed to return to the search for God by means of a friendship as special as is that found in the intimate exchange of prayer" (*Life*, p. 82).

Teresa had learned to pray as a young girl, and when she went through her serious illness, she began to consider more seriously the truths of faith and her own vocation. After her father's death in 1543, Teresa took as her confessor the Dominican Vicente Barrón. She talked about her troubles with prayer. Vicente advised her to hold fast to prayer because it would prove to be beneficial. Despite lapses, Teresa returned to prayer with new conviction. She began to sense that in some mysterious way it was no longer in her control to abandon prayer, for God held her in a divine hand and desired to give her greater favors.

For twenty years, Teresa voyaged on a tempestuous sea—neither enjoying God nor finding happiness in her world. When she experienced the enjoyments of the world, she felt sad because she remembered what she owed to God; when she turned to God, her attachments to things disturbed her.

At last, around the age of forty, Teresa experienced a conversion, a final integration of herself with the mystery of Christ. An image of Jesus in agony had been brought into the oratory of the convent for a special feast. Relying on the compassion of God for her and for all sinners, Teresa began to pray:

I strove to represent Christ within me, and it did me greater good—in my opinion—to represent Him in those scenes where I saw Him more alone. It seemed to me that being alone and afflicted, as a person in need, He had to accept me. (*Life*, p. 101)

With tears and dismay, with keen awareness of Christ's suffering for her sinfulness, and with remorse at her own ingratitude, Teresa placed all her trust in God: "I think I then said that I would not rise from there until He granted what I was begging Him for," to have the strength not to offend God again. "I believe certainly," she continued, "this was beneficial to me, because from that time I went on improving" (Life, p. 101).

The Reform Begins

As Teresa's conversion gained strength, she began to think about establishing Carmelite houses in which the primitive rule could be lived.

Discussions about this idea began in 1560. Teresa felt called to return to the simpler, quieter, more contemplative lifestyle of the early monks. Once, in a casual conversation, some remarked that if the sisters at the Incarnation could not live the simple life, perhaps another monastery could be founded. This idea took form in Teresa's mind. Soon she discussed the project with a friend—a wealthy widow—who began plans to provide a house for the new foundation.

At the same time, Teresa discovered that some of the other sisters had the same desire to lead a more enclosed, contemplative life. Still not sure if the project was a call from God, Teresa prayed fervently. Finally, God gave her an answer. According to Teresa, upon returning from Communion one day, God ordered her to found a new monastery. God promised to help her and told her to name the new house after St. Joseph, who would be the monastery's protector. Christ would dwell with the community, which would eventually be a light to all Christians. With God's call confirmed, Teresa knew that she must proceed to found Saint Joseph's Monastery.

The Founding of Saint Joseph's Monastery

Teresa's sister and brother-in-law bought the house that later became the Monastery of Saint Joseph. This was done with some secrecy because Teresa knew that many people in the city and the sisters of the Incarnation Monastery would be angered. People in the city would object to having to fund another monastery. The sisters would be affronted. Around this time, Teresa's brother-in-law became sick while his wife was away, and Teresa was mandated by her superiors to stay with him. Thus, when Saint Joseph's Monastery was opened, Teresa's move out of the Incarnation Monastery had already been accomplished.

The local bishop wanted the new monastery to be opened, but having seen the negative attitude of the local citizenry, the Carmelite provincial withdrew his permission. Teresa's Jesuit confessor and an influential Dominican priest encouraged her to keep pursuing her plan. Teresa held firm because of her conviction that God wanted the community to be established. Thus, in 1562, Teresa and several sisters, including newly received novices, opened Saint Joseph's.

Needless to say, Teresa's action caused an uproar. She was ordered back to the Incarnation, where she told her whole story to the prioress, who then wrote to the Carmelite provincial. The city council decided that the foundation should in no way be allowed to continue. Hearings were held in which the matter was debated. Teresa's Dominican friend was the only one to present a case on her behalf. A lawsuit commenced. Two years passed before the matters were finally settled: The new foundation was allowed its existence, and Teresa was given permission to live there.

Life at Saint Joseph's

Later in life, Teresa called the five years that she had lived at Saint Joseph's the most peaceful, calm, and quiet years of her life. In this period, the number of sisters at Saint Joseph's doubled.

The little group spent their days working, praying, renovating the house, expanding the garden, and, at times, extending hospitality. They owned no personal property and supported themselves with alms in return for their sewing and spinning. The sisters lived in strict enclosure. But Teresa encouraged a spirit of celebration among the sisters. Legends tell that on feast days, she handed out castanets so that the sisters could rejoice by dancing. One of her most famous sayings and a good piece of advice is, "God deliver us from sullen saints!" (McGinley, *Saint-Watching*, p. 93).

Teresa always maintained her sense of humor. For instance, a Sister once signed a letter, "one no better than dung." Teresa quipped that she hoped the Sister's humility was more than just talk. On another occasion, someone criticized Teresa for eating a partridge that someone had donated. Her reply was, "There is a time for partridge and a time for penance!" (Mary Reed Newland, *The Saint Book*, p. 164). As the years passed, Teresa's good humor was tested many times.

Visitors came to see for themselves what was happening at Saint Joseph's. On one occasion, a Franciscan friar, Alonso Maldonado, came to visit. Having recently returned from the Indies, he spoke to Teresa about missionary work and gave a conference to all the sisters. Moved by his talk about far-away places where there was much to be done, Teresa wept and prayed to be able to do something to help. While at prayer, she heard these comforting words: "Wait a little, daughter, and you will see great things" (*Foundations*, p. 102). These words did console Teresa, but their meaning became clear only many months later.

New Foundations, Continued Reforms

To Teresa's surprise, the superior general of the Carmelites came to visit the communities in Spain. No Carmelite superior general had ever visited Spain. Given the disapproval of the majority of Carmelites for her new monastery and its reforms, Teresa grew afraid that the superior, Fray Juan Bautista Rubeo de Ravena, would order her and the other sisters to go back to the Incarnation Monastery. Although Teresa did have the permission of her provincial superior and the bishop to maintain Saint Joseph's, she did not have that of the superior general.

Teresa invited the Father General to Saint Joseph's, and with some trepidation, she gave him a truthful and open account of the events. She also gave him an account of her soul and told him her life story. To Teresa's great relief, he encouraged her and assured her that he would not order her to leave Saint Joseph's. The superior went even further; he gave Teresa "patent letters" so that she could found new monasteries of the strict observance. These letters would override the objections of any local superior. Subsequent to this, Teresa also asked for and received the Father General's permission to begin monasteries for the friars in which the primitive rule would be kept.

Having the permissions and the will was one thing, but actually founding new houses required money and support. Years later, Teresa wrote,

Here I was, a poor discalced [shoeless] nun, without help from anywhere—only from the Lord—weighed down with patent letters and good desires, and without there being any possibility of my getting the work started. Neither courage nor hope failed, for since the Lord had given the one thing, He would give the other. Everything now seemed very possible, and so I set to work. "O greatness of

God! How you manifest Your power in giving courage to an ant!" (*Foundations*, p. 105)

Like those of a worker ant, Teresa's efforts proved prodigious. Over the years ahead, she opened seventeen monasteries for women and founded a network of monasteries for men.

To travel between her foundations, Teresa walked or rode cranky mules and springless carts. Her health was never robust, but she carried on with faith and wit. An incident that was typical of Teresa's life happened to her on a trip to Seville. As Teresa and her Sister-companions made their way to the city, Teresa came down with a dangerous fever. The sisters "stormed heaven" for help and doused her face with water. Because the sun was scorching, the water did little good. A windowless room in flea-ridden inn added to Teresa's illness. The sun turned it into an oven; the lumpy uneven bed prevented sleep. Eventually, Teresa decided to leave the inn, preferring to lie in an open field instead. She concluded, "What a thing sickness is! For when we're healthy, it's easy to put up with all kinds of inconveniences. . . . The Lord was pleased that the severity of the fever did not last beyond that day" (*Foundations*, p. 225). Obviously, God had called Teresa to share in the human and social conditions of her day. She did so with continued goodwill.

Teresa was a mystic, but she was also intensely practical. For instance, sound advice on everything from choice of cloth for stockings to treatments for various ailments filled her letters. To open houses, she had to negotiate with civil and church authorities who did not always treat her with respect. Waiting for necessary permissions from them demanded tact, firmness, patience and determination.

Teresa's preferred mode of moving into a new foundation was to arrive after sunset, spend several hours cleaning and setting up the household (and resting if possible), and then have Mass said at dawn so that the Blessed Sacrament would already be in residence before the townspeople started their day. This seemed to forestall local commotion and minimize the sisters' inconvenience. After all, for those who are called to solitude, being outside their own houses was—as Teresa once said—like being fish out of water. Sometimes moving into a new foundation this way worked smoothly. At other times, it did not go as well.

In 1570, on All Saints' Day, Teresa arrived with a companion at Salamanca. The house deeded for them had been occupied by university students who had resisted eviction up to the last moment. The sisters entered the house at night. In looking around, Teresa noted that the students did not have a penchant for cleanliness. Her companion worried that some of the angry students might still be there. So the sisters locked themselves in a room and slept on two borrowed blankets thrown over some straw. Teresa's companion, fretting about the possibility of lurking students, evidently kept Teresa awake. Her apprehension aroused Teresa's own fears. The sonorous tolling of the church bells increased the anxiety in the darkened room. Finally, a fatigued Teresa—realizing the ruse to which she was falling prey—told her companion to let her sleep; she would worry about the situation in the morning. The following day more sisters came and their anxieties evaporated.

Teresa knew the difficulties involved in establishing a house, but she also knew the satisfaction and fulfillment that came when the process was completed. In addition, she received joy from many friendships. Perhaps her best-known friend was St. John of the Cross, one of the first two friars to join her movement to open reformed houses of men. John, a mystic and poet, also held his ground against strong opposition to reform. At one point, the non-reformed provincial had John imprisoned for nine months at Toledo. His friend Teresa prayed and worried until John escaped.

Teresa's Writings

We know Teresa mainly through the extant copies of her own writings. The first of these is *The Book of Her Life,* written at the direction of her confessor García de Toledo to give an account of the graces of her interior life. It is a mix of recounted events and descriptions of prayer. Because the manuscript was initially given to her confessor and reputedly then to a council of the Inquisition, Teresa wrote another book on prayer for her Carmelite sisters, entitled *The Way of Perfection.* Many years later, she wrote *The Interior Castle,* which deals with the same subject in a more systematic fashion and with a mature, peaceful spirit.

The Book of Her Foundations provides a delightful account of the incidents and events of Teresa's life. This book not only covers the beginnings of each of the houses of the primitive rule but also spontaneously speaks of people who were dear to Teresa.

Teresa authored smaller works also, such as *Mediations on the Song of Songs, The Constitutions*, and some poetry. Happily, much of Teresa's correspondence escaped destruction and is bound in several volumes. The vast number of Teresa's books, plus her volumes of letters, explain why she complained about not having enough time to spend on her spinning.

The Close of Teresa's Life

The account of the end of Teresa's life comes from Ana de San Bartolomé, who had been Teresa's nurse and secretary since 1577—when Teresa had broken her arm. In 1582, after a wearying year of travel and conflict, sickness, and continuous planning, Teresa and Ana came to Alba de Tormes. After September 29, Teresa never left her bed. A severe hemorrhage drained away her last resources. On October 1, the sisters elected a prioress. Teresa stayed aloof from their deliberations, knowing that from then on they would have to act without her.

On October 3, Teresa asked that Communion and the last sacraments be brought to her. The following day, the feast of St. Francis of Assisi, Teresa was tranquil. She died in the evening.

While love is sweet,

Long awaiting is not.

Because in dying

My hope in living in assured.

(Teresa, *Poetry*, in *The Collected Works of St. Teresa of Ávila*, vol. 3, p. 376)

TERESA'S SPIRITUALITY

Intimacy with Scripture

Teresa's spirituality is replete with texts, references, and images from Scripture. As did Ignatius of Loyola in this same century in Spain, Teresa entered—with sense and imagination, with thought and affection—into the mysteries she contemplated in the Scriptures.

In her poetry, Teresa appeals to the symbolism of both the Hebrew and the Christian Scriptures. For instance, she writes,

Calvary of Tabor give me,

Desert or fruitful land;

As Job in suffering

Or John at Your breast;

Barren or fruited vine,

Whatever be Your will:

What do You want of me?

Be I Joseph chained
Or as Egypt's governor,
David pained
Or exalted high,
Jonas drowned,
Or Jonas freed:
What do You want of me?
(*Poetry*, pp. 378–379)

In this passage, Teresa identifies herself completely with figures and situations from Scripture. They are more than a metaphor for her: Poetically, Teresa is at the place of crucifixion and on the mount of the Transfiguration; she is with Job on the dunghill and with John at the Last Supper.

Teresa and Prayer

Teresa compares prayer to watering a garden. Getting the water may or may not be laborious. One way is to lower the bucket into a well and then to raise the bucket and carry its limited contents to the garden. A second way employs a windlass that carries the bucket to the surface of the water. A third way channels rivulets from a stream to the garden. And the final way is to let the rains come. In other words, like watering a garden, prayer can take many forms—from determined activity to grateful satisfaction. The important thing is that the garden gets watered.

As a child, Teresa frequently withdrew into solitude to pray the rosary, a prayer form taught to her by her mother. As a young person, Teresa engaged in vocal prayer that awakened her attention to God. For Teresa, vocal prayer was a form of mental prayer—prayer that made her "mindful."

Throughout her life, Teresa found discursive prayer difficult. Without some aid to keep her thoughts from wandering, she found concentration hard. Even using her imagination in prayer proved to be problematic.

Teresa always liked to read. So when she began prayer with the assistance of a book, she found it easier to address her thoughts and feelings to God and to let herself be addressed by God. Reading a book was like using a bucket; it was a tool to engage her mind and her heart in a dialog. Later, a quiet presence would set in, and the stream would flow gently.

Nature caught Teresa's eye and spoke to her heart. Looking at fields of grain, water, or blooming flowers helped Teresa become mindful of God the Creator.

Finally, in her companions, Teresa found motivation, correction, and sustenance for her prayer.

Devotion to the Saints

Throughout her life, Teresa was devoted to the saints. She saw them as models of a virtuous life and as friends who would intercede on her behalf. Particular favorites of Teresa's were Mary Magdalene, Martha and Mary, and St. Joseph.

Teresa turned to St. Joseph as an advocate when she was ill in 1542. Seeing the helplessness of the doctors around her, she was determined to seek the aid of this saint. Though patient with her sickness, Teresa desired her health. She attributed her eventual recovery to St. Joseph. Indeed, Teresa frequently appealed to St. Joseph for all manner of aid.

Central Themes in Teresa's Spirituality

Humility: The foundation of Teresa's spirituality is humility, the virtue of accepting reality as it is, including human reality. Humility counters arrogance and melancholy. Humble acts like sweeping the floor, speaking with a confessor, going for a walk in the country, and eating and sleeping in reasonable proportion are the remedy for both self-aggrandizement and self-deprecation.

Obedience: Obedience was Teresa's response to the word of God. Sometimes, this was obedience to the word heard within her. At other times, she obeyed the word given to her or confirmed for her by someone in a position of legitimate authority. Teresa believed that by obeying the word of God promptly and with perseverance, and by taking on responsibilities, people formed their destinies according to God's will.

Courage and determination: Teresa was well aware of obstacles to an intimate life with God—both within herself and within her mission. She often spoke of herself as a "miserable creature," that is, one in need of mercy. Courage was necessary to endure the physical ailments that accompanied her throughout her life, to move beyond self-doubts that were awakened by an adversarial spirit, and to carry out the work of foundation despite calumny and slander.

Love: Teresa's love for God was a reverent but spontaneous spousal love. It was a union and a relation of exchange with both God's humanity and divinity. Intimately connected to Teresa's love for God was the love she experienced for and with other people. The reciprocal love Teresa developed with other people deepened her love for God and flowed from her spiritual life.

TERESA FOR TODAY

In our own complex times, Teresa shows us what it means to be people alive in our own culture, people who enter into the depths of our own life and heart and find God there. She draws us into the web of personal relationships with friends, relatives, superiors, peers, and incidental acquaintances. She shows us that in the flow of life, we can take special care of our immediate situation, while faithfully keeping sight of the grand vision, the saving action of the loving God in all of life.

The Interior Castle

Theme: For Teresa, the soul is like an interior castle. The goal of the spiritual journey is to be united with God, who resides in the inmost center.

Opening prayer: God of glory, let me know your presence in me.

ABOUT TERESA

In 1577, Teresa wrote one of her major works, *The Interior Castle*. Composed near the end of her life, this book represents the culmination of Teresa's spiritual experience. Teresa attempted to explain the beauty of the inner life of the soul, the stages in a life of prayer, and the characteristic joys and trials of each stage.

Teresa pictured the soul as a beautiful mansion in which God resides in the centermost place. This interior castle contains seven dwelling places. We start our spiritual journey in the most exterior dwelling (the first) and, God willing, move toward the seventh. A person enters this seventh dwelling—one's own center—only when God allows it. In the innermost dwelling, the person becomes united with God in continuous, conscious love.

As Teresa began writing *The Interior Castle*, she struggled to find the best image that she could think of for representing the soul. She prayed that God would give her the words to best express the truth of what she wanted to say. Eventually, the image of the interior castle came to her mind:

> . . . We consider our soul to be like a castle made entirely out of a diamond or of very clear crystal, in which there are many rooms, just as in heaven there are many dwelling places. For in reflecting upon it carefully, Sisters, we realize that the soul of the just person is nothing else but a paradise where the Lord says He finds His delight. (*The Collected Works of St. Teresa of Ávila*, vol. 2, p. 283)

Pause: Reflect on what God's indwelling presence means to you and on what image best represents God's presence.

TERESA'S WORDS

I don't find anything comparable to the magnificent beauty of a soul and its marvelous capacity. Indeed, our intellects, however keen, can hardly comprehend it, just as they cannot comprehend God; but He himself says that He created us in His own image and likeness. . . .

It is a shame and unfortunate that through our own fault we don't understand ourselves or know who we are.

Wouldn't it show great ignorance, my daughters, if someone when asked who he was didn't know, and didn't know his father or mother or from what country he came? Well now, if this would be so extremely stupid, we are incomparably more so when we do not strive to know who we are, but limit ourselves to considering only roughly these bodies. Because we have heard and because faith tells us so, we know we have souls. But we seldom consider the precious things that can be found in this soul, or who dwells within it, or its high value. Consequently, little effort is made to preserve its beauty. All of our attention is taken up with the plainness of the diamond's setting or the outer wall of the castle; that is, with these bodies of ours.

Well, let us consider that this castle has, as I said, many dwelling places: some up above, others down below, others to the sides; and in the center and the middle is the main dwelling place where the very secret exchanges between God and the soul take place. (*Interior Castle*, pp. 283–84)

REFLECTION

Today, as in Teresa's time, external affairs and realities can very easily lure us into ignoring our own soul. Even when we acknowledge that fact (or the possibility) that we may possess a soul, we rarely think of entering into it, or we candidly admit we do not know quite how to do this.

For Teresa, the door of entry into the soul was prayer and reflection. And those who start to practice prayer often experience a strange exhilaration, a new peace, a more vivid life. As with any exercise, prayer may seem laborious and unproductive at the beginning. But once beyond these beginnings, a new realm of intimacy, resourcefulness, and security gradually manifests itself. God invites us toward the center of our interior castle.

❧ Teresa spoke of the soul as a castle or a garden in which God takes delight. How do you allow God to delight in you? Dialog with God about the delight you find in yourself as God's friend. How do you celebrate the delight that you find in your soul? If you have not expressed delight in God's presence in your soul, perhaps you can hum, sing, or whistle a favorite hymn of praise or thanksgiving. Do not worry about the quality of your voice, the strength of your whistle, or even about your ability to remember the song's lyrics. Just hum, sing, or whistle, knowing that God is in your soul and enjoys your recognition of God's presence.

❧ In early stages of prayer, we may become bogged down in what Teresa called "a mud of fears." Instead of being able to relate to God, our fears clog our attention.

Let your mind explore. Ask yourself what some of your fears are, and write a list or a description of your fears. Then write about how these fears affect your emotional and spiritual life.

Next, sit quietly. Close your eyes. Put your fears aside for a moment and concentrate on your slow, deep, rhythmic breathing. Relax.

≀♠ As you continue to breathe slowly in and out, imagine the deepest part of your soul as a wonderful garden or a room, the innermost place in your interior castle. This place is filled with light, warmth, security, and love. See, hear, and feel this place in your soul where you meet the loving God.

As you draw close to God, take off your fears also. Offer each fear to God. Ask God to free you, to wash away your fears. Then, walk into the water, allowing it to refresh and cleanse you. Let all tensions go. Thank God for this baptismal cleansing.

Hear God's response: "Be not afraid. I am with you." Repeat these words softly over and over in a prayer.

≀♠ Use Jesus' name as a repeated prayer.

≀♠ With soft music playing in the background, sketch on paper or model in clay an image that depicts the indwelling of God in your soul.

GOD'S WORD

If you remain in me and my words remain in you, you may ask for whatever you please and you will get it. It is to the glory of my Father that you should bear much fruit and be my disciples. I have loved you just as the Father has loved me. Remain in my love. If you keep my commandments you will remain in my love, just as I have kept my Father's commandments and remain in his love. I have told you this so that my own joy may be in you and your joy be complete. (John 15:7-11)

Closing prayer: Life-giving God, I believe that you are ever dwelling within me. Draw me to yourself in light and love. Teach me to walk happily in all my inner spaces.

Beginning to Pray

Theme: As we begin a heartfelt conversation with God, we become aware of both the freeing power of grace and the crippling effects of sin.

Opening prayer: O loving Creator, heal me with your resounding word and your gentle spirit.

ABOUT TERESA

In her writings on beginning to pray, Teresa spoke of the soul as being crippled or even paralyzed. Having been paralyzed herself, Teresa understood that relearning to coordinate one's own movement comes gradually and only with painstaking effort that initially may be difficult and seem unrewarding. Beginning to pray may be difficult and seem unrewarding too, but is therapy for the paralyzed soul.

Teresa wrote about a wise man who told her once that people who do not pray regularly are like paralytics. Despite having hands and feet, they cannot direct the movements of these limbs.

Teresa recalled the passage in John's gospel (5:1-9) concerning Jesus' healing of the lame man. In this story, the movement beyond paralysis comes as a grace of God. This is true of inner paralysis also. Healing may come early in life, or it may come after many years, depending on one's training, desires, and the freely given gifts of God. But prayer establishes the contact with God, the source of all healing for body or soul. Teresa assumed that we would always be delighted in the experience of God's enabling grace.

Pause: Recall the experience of prayer in which you were aware of the presence of God bringing you inner freedom.

Teresa's Words

Whoever has not begun the practice of prayer, I beg for the love of the Lord not to go without so great a good. There is nothing here to fear but only something to desire. Even if there be no great progress, or much effort in reaching such perfection as to deserve the favor and mercies God bestows on the more generous, at least a person will come to understand the road leading to heaven. And if one perseveres, I trust then in the mercy of God, who never fails to repay anyone who has taken Him for a friend. For mental prayer in my opinion is nothing else than an intimate sharing between friends; it means taking time frequently to be alone with Him who we know loves us. (*Life*, p. 96)

REFLECTION

Teresa's writings affirm, according to the traditions of the church, that God offers all humans the graces they need for salvation. One of these graces is the gift of prayer in which we enter into ourselves and speak to God, who loves us. Like any friendship, friendship with God takes initial effort, time, and personal presence. In this relationship, we may become aware of our weaknesses, our inabilities, and our destructive propensities. At the same time, we can come to realize that a new mode of life is beckoning and attracting us.

❧ Teresa posed some questions that are worth reflecting on in this age of information and verbiage but of less communication:

Do I approach personal prayer as an attempt to speak to God, the one who loves me?

Do I allow myself to become discouraged when I feel inept in expressing myself to God?

Do I avoid prayer because it seems so unreal?

❧ Reflect on the quality of the conversations in your daily life: your way of getting another person's attention, your tone of voice, your sincerity about being heard, the content of your message, your ability to hear another person, and the verbal or nonverbal gestures that you use to close the conversation. Continue this reflection by examining how others communicate with you. Write a summary of these considerations.

Next, reflect on the way you approach and speak with God and on the way God approaches and speaks with you.

Do you speak with God like you speak with other people?

Are your expectations the same or different?

Do you find yourself trying to hide aspects of your life from God?

Do you tiptoe around issues with God the way you might tiptoe around issues with other people? Is this necessary?

End this reflection by talking with God about the relationship and communication that you share. Ask God to send you whatever you need in order to deepen and enliven your relationship.

❧ In what areas of your spiritual or emotional life do you find yourself paralyzed or crippled? Find a friend to talk to about this, or write a letter to yourself explaining the whole situation. Finally, offer these areas of paralysis to God. Discuss them. Maybe you will be healed or find release soon, maybe not. Can you rest in God's hands with or without remedy?

❧ Trusting in the mercy of God, take time and find a space to be alone with the One who loves you. Speak your mind and heart; listen with your mind and heart.

❧ Meditate on the passage from John's gospel in "God's Word." Imagine yourself as the one with whom Jesus is speaking.

GOD'S WORD

After this there was a Jewish festival, and Jesus went up to Jerusalem. Now in Jerusalem next to the Sheep Pool there is a pool called Bethesda in Hebrew, which has five porticos; and under these were crowds of sick people, blind, lame, paralyzed. One man there had an illness which had lasted thirty-eight years, and when Jesus saw him lying there and knew he had been in that condition for a long time, he said, "Do you want to be well again?" "Sir," replied the sick man, "I have no one to put me into the pool when the water is disturbed; and while I am still on the way, someone else gets down there before me." Jesus said, "Get up, pick up your sleeping-mat and walk around." The man was cured at once, and he picked up his mat and started to walk around. (John 5:1-9)

Closing prayer: God, you know my heart. When I hear your voice, I realize that I am sometimes too broken to respond. In your mercy, heal me. Let me walk. Let me walk around in the temple of my soul and in the temple of your world.

MEDITATION THREE

Good Conversations

Theme: God speaks to and heals our souls through good conversations with our friends, family members, counselors, and spiritual directors.

Opening prayer: My God, teach me to talk and listen so that your healing grace may be at work in me.

ABOUT TERESA

Teresa believed that in the early stages of prayer, God often speaks to people in and through good conversations with their friends. In her own life, Teresa had ongoing conversations with many men and women—spiritual directors, religious superiors, friends, relations, and sundry others.

In *The Book of Her Foundations*, Teresa wrote about her early acquaintance with a man who later became one of the first reformed Carmelite friars. During a visit to Medina, Teresa sought the advice of the prior of the Carmelite monastery there. She wanted to found reformed monasteries for men but did not know how to begin.

[The prior] was happy to know of it and promised me he would be the first. I took it that he was joking with me and told him so. For although he was always a good friar, recollected, very studious, and fond of his cell—in fact, he was a learned man—it didn't seem to me he was the one for a beginning like this. Neither would he have the courage or promote the austerity that was necessary, since he was fragile and not given to austerity.

The prior confided to Teresa that he strongly desired to lead a more regular monastic life. In fact, he planned to join the Carthusians. Teresa continued:

Despite all this, I was not completely satisfied. Although I was happy to hear what he said, I asked that we put it off for a while and that he prepare by putting into practice the things he would be promising. And this he did. . . . (p. 112)

In various situations, Teresa spontaneously sensed that conversations were an appropriate way to discover the will of God. They were a source of consolation and discernment. Often they carried love in them. She regularly took her conversations to prayer, and her prayer to conversations.

Pause: Reflect on conversations you have had that were sources for discerning the presence of God.

TERESA'S WORDS

One day I was wondering if it was an attachment for me to find satisfaction in being with persons with whom I discuss my soul and whom I love, or with those who I see are great servants of God since it consoled me to be with them. The Lord told me that if a sick person who was in danger of death thought a doctor was bringing about a cure, that sick person wouldn't be virtuous for failing to thank and love the doctor; that if it hadn't been for these persons what would I have done; that conversation with good persons is not harmful, but that my words should always be well weighed and holy, and that I shouldn't fail to converse with them; that doing so is beneficial rather than harmful. This consoled me greatly because sometimes, since conversing with them seemed to me to be an attachment, I didn't want to talk to them at all. (*Life*, pp. 360–361)

REFLECTION

Although Teresa sometimes alluded to the wastefulness and danger of frivolous conversation, she regularly encouraged her sisters to disclose the movements of their souls to other people. Throughout her life, Teresa herself enjoyed such conversation. For her, the content of the conversation was not always as important as the benefits of good, open talk—bonding between the communicators, securing of the soul in the will of God, and consolation—both human and divine.

Teresa noted, through, that some of her conversations left her uneasy. In these instances, she often needed a second round of talk or an ongoing discussion. Perhaps for all of us, conversation is an art that needs to be learned. It is not always easy to talk with someone else and to really listen to them.

Conversation about the things of God is both easier and harder than other conversations—easier because the word of God, heard through books and letters and human sharing, truly can touch our heart and attract our mind; harder because we may find ourselves mute in response, stammering and inept in our own speaking.

As we begin to disclose our souls, we may discover within ourselves grace and sin—both of which resist the light of mutual presence. But during conversations in which we open our soul to a confidant, the Spirit is present—purifying and consoling, cleansing and satisfying.

&. Write down the names of four people who have been important to you in your life with God. Recall the most important thing each one has said to you and write that down next to their name. Praise God for their presence in your life.

&. Recall a particularly important conversation that you have had, a conversation that helped you come to an important decision or that marked some turning point in your life. In order to meditate on this conversation, close your eyes. Relax. Speak the name of the person with whom you had this key talk and bring to mind the face of this person. Then, recall the scene of your talk. Re-create your conversation. Go through it completely—words, feelings—all of it.

After the conversation is over, ponder in your heart these questions:

What effects did this conversation have on me?

Looking back, what was God saying to me in this conversation?

Was I aware at the time that God could and did speak through the other person?

Finally, talk to God about this important conversation and the person with whom you conversed.

᪥ Take a walk with or go visit a friend. Talk about something that is important to you in living your life of faith.

᪥ Recall two conversations that you have had recently—one that was rewarding and one that was not. Then contrast the two conversations in terms of the situation, the topics, the personal presence of the communicators, the level of honesty, and the importance in your relationship.

How did your own participation contribute to the rewards of the first conversation and the lack of rewards in the other conversation?

What attitudes toward conversing with other people help you?

Do you need to change other attitudes, so that when you have conversations you can more fully be the presence of Christ to other people?

Converse with God about this matter; bring to God your sorrow, happiness, desires, and petitions.

☙ Meditate on the passage from Luke in "God's Word." Reflect on the conversation and feelings of the disciples on the way to Emmaus. Write down the feeling that is the most vivid for you in this sequence of events.

GOD'S WORD

Now that very same day, two of them were on their way to a village called Emmaus, seven miles from Jerusalem, and they were talking together about all that had happened. And it happened that as they were talking together and discussing it, Jesus himself came up and walked by their side; but their eyes were prevented from recognizing him. He said to them, "What are all these things that you are discussing as you walk along?" They stopped, their faces downcast.

Then one of them, called Cleopas, answered him, "You must be the only person staying in Jerusalem who does not know the things that have been happening there these last few days."

[Jesus] asked, "What things?" They answered, "All about Jesus of Nazareth, who showed himself [to be] a prophet powerful in action and speech before God and the whole people; and how our chief priests and our leaders handed him over to be sentenced to death, and had him crucified. Our own hope had been that he would be the one to set Israel free. And this is not all: two whole days have now gone by since it all happened; and some women from our group have astounded us: they went to the tomb in the early morning, and when they could not find the body, they came back to tell us [that] they had seen a vision of angels who declared he was alive. Some of our friends went to the tomb and found everything exactly as the women had reported, but of him they saw nothing."

Then [Jesus] said to them, "You foolish men! So slow to believe all that the prophets have said! Was it not necessary that the Christ should suffer before entering into his glory?" Then, starting with Moses and going through all the prophets, he explained to them the passages throughout the scriptures that were about himself.

When they drew near to the village to which they were going, he made as if to go on; but they pressed him to stay with them saying, "It is nearly evening, and the day is almost over." So he went in to stay with them. Now while he was with them at table, he took the bread and said the blessing; then he broke it and handed it to them. And their eyes were opened and they recognized him; but he had vanished from their sight. Then they said to each other, "Did not our hearts burn within us as he talked to us on the road and explained the scriptures to us?"

They set out that instant and returned to Jerusalem. There they found the Eleven assembled together with their companions, who said to them, "The Lord has indeed risen and has appeared to Simon." Then they told their story of what had happened on the road and how they had recognized him at the breaking of bread. (Luke 24:13-35)

Closing prayer: God of our life, thank you for the ability to hear and to speak, to listen and to talk. Let us be hearers and speakers of your word. May your Spirit continue to console and enlighten us in our conversations.

Spiritual Transformation

Theme: In the spiritual life, we do well to expect our transformation to come in stages and to trust in God during the process.

Opening prayer: Creating and saving God, give me the discernment to know which stage of my spiritual life I am in and to be content with that insofar as it is according to your goodwill.

ABOUT TERESA

In her writings, Teresa always groped for images with which to explain spiritual truths. One of her best-known images for spiritual growth or transformation is that of the silkworm at its birth, in its active caterpillar state, in its cocoon form, and in its butterfly stage. Our spiritual transformation is analogous to the changes of the silkworm:

> You must have already heard about His marvels manifested in the way silk originates, for only He could have invented something like that. The silkworms come from seeds about the size of little grains of pepper. . . . When the warm weather comes and the leaves begin to appear on

the mulberry tree, the seeds start to live, for they are dead until then. The worms nourish themselves on mulberry leaves until, having grown to full size, they settle on some twigs. There with their little mouths they themselves go about spinning the silk and making some very thick little cocoons in which they enclose themselves. The silkworm, which is fat and ugly, then dies, and a little white butterfly, which is very pretty, comes forth from the cocoon. Now if this were not seen but recounted to us as having happened in other times, who would believe it? Or what reasonings could make us conclude that a thing as nonrational as a worm or a bee could be so diligent in working for our benefit and with so much industriousness? And the poor little worm loses its life in the challenge. This is enough, Sisters, for a period of meditation even through I may say no more to you; in it you can consider the wonders and the wisdom of our God. (*Interior Castle*, pp. 341–342)

With the silkworm image, Teresa affirms the identity of the soul in the hand of God, the vast differences of each stage of spiritual growth, and the change of form that takes place. While the natural phenomenon of the silkworm's transformation is astonishing, the transformation of the spirit is so subtle and wonderful that it can only be understood partially and by comparison.

Pause: Ponder the wonder of the transforming silkworm.

Teresa's Words

You must note that there are different kinds of sufferings. Some sufferings are produced suddenly by our human nature, and the same goes for consolations, and even by the charity of compassion for one's neighbor, as our Lord experienced when He raised Lazarus. Being united with God's will doesn't take these experiences away, not do they disturb the soul with a restless, disquieting passion that lasts a long while. These sufferings pass quickly. As I have said concerning consolations in prayer, it seems they do not reach the soul's depth but only the senses and faculties. . . .

Nonetheless, take careful note, daughters, that it is necessary for the silkworm to die, and, moreover, at a cost to yourselves. In the delightful union, the experience of seeing oneself in so new a life greatly helps one to die. . . .

This union with God's will is the union I have desired all my life; it is the union I ask the Lord for always and the one that is clearest and safest. (*Interior Castle*, pp. 349–350)

Reflection

In using the image of the silkworm, the cocoon, and the white butterfly, Teresa wanted to help her sisters understand that the soul's life with God follows stages, which are brought to awareness during prayer. She wanted to encourage, console, and strengthen the sisters. She wanted to alleviate misplaced anxieties and unnecessary feelings of guilt that often surface in times of transition from one stage to another or when a person seems stuck in a rut.

One of the traits of humility is to recognize and live in the stage that is true to us and to do the work that is given us to do. The caterpillar cannot fly; it eats. The butterfly no longer creeps; it need not spin silk. Teresa helps us to recognize that there are differing possibilities in each stage.

One aspect of discernment is the ability to recognize who and what we really are and what we can and cannot do, and to live contentedly, knowing that God will call us to grow, to move into new stages, to be transformed—even by passing through a death. Those who believe in Christ live in hope of a final beauty and freedom that God will bring about in us.

🍃 Go for a walk and find some tiny, magnificent creature or object that is a sign of God's creating and transforming power for you today. Reflect on the many things in your surroundings that are undergoing transformative change. You may want to write a list of all these things. Then, thank God for each one.

🍃 Ponder the things a caterpillar, a caterpillar in a cocoon, and a butterfly can and cannot do. Identify the stage that most describes your spiritual life at present. Rest in the presence of the Creator, who knows and loves you and, in the Spirit's own mysterious way, governs the stage you are in.

❧ Talk with God about the stage of your growth and speak the words of "The Serenity Prayer": "God, grant me the serenity to accept the things I cannot change, courage to change the things I can, and the wisdom to know the difference."

In what way are you "making silk" for other people out of your own labor and your own self?

How is this causing your "death" (e.g., fatigue, nonpossession of self, death to sin, and so on)?

How is your "silk-making" contributing to the social good of this world and the persons in it?

GOD'S WORD

It is as scripture says: What no eye has seen and no ear has heard, what the mind of man cannot vizualise; all that God has prepared for those who love him; to us, though, God has given revelation through the Spirit, for the Spirit explores the depths of everything, even the depths of God. After all, is there anyone who knows the qualities of anyone except his own spirit, within him; and in the same way, nobody knows the qualities of God except the Spirit of God. Now, the Spirit we have received is not the spirit of the world but God's own Spirit, so that we may understand the lavish gifts God has given us. (1 Corinthians 2:9-12)

Closing prayer:

> When at last
> You enter my heart,
> My God, then at once
> I fear your leaving.
> (Teresa, *Poetry*, p. 384)

Divine Providence

Theme: The mystery of God's action calls us to be alert and responsive to the unexpected events that happen in our life.

Opening prayer: Ever-active God, teach me to receive the unexpected events in my life as signs of your presence. Help me to read them as workings of your will.

ABOUT TERESA

In writing *The Book of Her Foundations*, Teresa made evident her belief in the providence of God. She believed that if God wanted the houses of reformed Carmelites founded, they would be founded. For example, Teresa told the following story:

Once, when she was at her wits' end, something unexpected happened. At Mass one day, a poor young man by the name of Andrada approached Teresa. He told her that his spiritual director, Franciscan friar Martín de La Cruz, had sent him and that he stood prepared to help her in any way that he could. Teresa wrote: "I thanked him and was amused, and my companions even more so, to see the kind of help that saintly man had sent us. The clothes this young man had on were not the kind one would wear when going to speak with discalced nuns" (p. 171).

But Teresa did have a problem. Even though she had a permit to open a new house, she could not find a suitable dwelling. None of her influential friends had any leads. Then she recalled Andrada's offer of assistance. Teresa continued with her story, reflecting on the various notions that were playing in her consciousness. Upon mentioning Andrada to the other sisters,

> they laughed very much at me and told me not to do such a thing, that it would serve for no more than to make the secret plan public. I didn't want to listen to them. Since he was sent by that servant of God, I trusted that there was something for him to do and that his offer to help had a mystery about it. (pp. 171–172)

Teresa asked Andrada to find a house for her to rent. She confirmed that she could guarantee payment. Andrada calmly assured her that he would find a proper place. A couple of days later, Andrada returned with keys in hand to a house nearby. The dwelling proved to be ideal, and the community opened. Reflecting on this event, Teresa remarked:

> Frequently, when I reflect on this foundation, I am amazed by the designs of God. For almost three months—at

least more than two, but I don't remember exactly—very wealthy persons had made the rounds of Toledo looking for a house for us and were never able to find one, as though there were no houses in the city. And then this youth comes along, not rich but very poor, and the Lord desired that he find one immediately. (p. 172)

Pause: Ponder this question: Have I ever recognized God's providence in the unexpected events of my life?

TERESA'S WORDS

I haven't experienced any promise in prayer that I haven't seen fulfilled, even though the promise may have come many years previously. There are so many things I see and understand about the grandeurs of God, and of His providence, that almost any time I begin to think about it my intellect fails me, as when one sees things that are far beyond one's ability to understand; and I remain in recollection. (*Spiritual Testimonies*, in *The Collected Works of St. Teresa of Ávila*, vol. 1, p. 385)

REFLECTION

As Teresa both lived and prayed, she learned to be attentive to all happenings as signs of the providence of God. She learned to trust and to use unexpected help to further what she understood as God's will for her, for the Carmelite community, and for reforming the Catholic church.

Teresa was able to read events, both successes and setbacks, as part of the workings of God's plan and as a fulfillment of the promises of Christ.

She mastered both the determination and the patience needed to deal with friends, enemies, and multiple levels of human systems—including religious authorities, civic councils, licensing boards, and neighbors. With zeal, forthrightness, political shrewdness, and humor, Teresa made decisions, planned as well as she could, and ultimately relied on a loving God to see her through the good and bad times.

Recall a time when someone who was poorly dressed (according to social norms) approached you or knocked at your door.

What were your spontaneous reactions?

Can you, like Teresa, laugh at your own reactions when something surprising like this happens?

Can you see God's providence in such times?

Pose these questions for your reflection and meditation on young people:

When a young man or a young woman enters my life, how often do I wonder, What can they do? Are they capable of anything?

Am I as open as Teresa was to discerning beneficial, even providential, opportunities in unexpected occurrences?

Am I free enough to call upon young people's talents and energies? Am I willing to admit that they may have more knowledge and even competency in some things than I do or than many of my adult friends and colleagues do?

Am I willing to accept their goodwill and employ their capabilities?

❧ Think of a young person you know. Reflect on their appearance, their style of approaching life, their goodwill and talents, their adolescent habits, and the general reactions of adults to them. Pray for them throughout the day.

❧ Reflect on your own reactions to the unexpected occurrences in your life. First jot down some unexpected events—a flat tire, the closing of a school or corporate office, the illness of a family member, and so on. Then choose one of these and write down your immediate reactions to the event. Give the event further consideration, and write your reactions to these questions:

How did God act in this unexpected event?

Did I look for God's will in this event?

Finally, write a prayer that enables you to weave this event into your awareness of the providence of God.

🍃 Reflect on an event in your life in which you needed and relied on both discretion from and trust in others. Pray for these persons in thanksgiving for who they are and for what they did on your behalf.

🍃 Pray repeatedly the words, "Loving God, teach me trust."

GOD'S WORD

In hope, we already have salvation; in hope, not visibly present, or we should not be hoping—nobody goes on hoping for something which is already visible. But having this hope for what we cannot yet see, we are able to wait for it with persevering confidence.

And as well as this, the Spirit too comes to help us in our weakness, for, when we do not know how to pray properly, then the Spirit personally makes our petitions for us in groans that cannot be put into words; and he who can see into all hearts knows what the Spirit means because the prayers that the Spirit makes for God's holy people are always in accordance with the mind of God. We are well aware that God works with those who love him, those who have been called in accordance with his purpose, and turns everything to their good. (Romans 8:24-28)

Closing prayer: Faithful God, I give you thanks for your providence at work in my life. Thank you especially for the unexpected events that show me your presence.

MEDITATION SIX

Courage

Theme: Courage is the virtue that moves us from being weak-souled (pusillanimous) to being great-souled (magnanimous). It enables us to overcome obstacles to doing the work of the saving God in this world.

Opening prayer: God of mercy and compassion, strengthen my heart so that I may be able to do what pleases you.

ABOUT TERESA

Teresa was attentive to her world, both within herself and outside herself. She often alluded to her weaknesses, fears, and vacillations. Yet Teresa knew that she was called to move beyond these, not only in her thoughts, but also in her actions. *Courage* and *determination* were important words for Teresa. The equanimity with which she accepted the hazards of travel was a reflection of her deep courage.

On a trip to Seville by wagon, Teresa and her companions were crossing the Guadalquivir River on a barge. The current proved to be too strong for those pulling the barge by rope from the opposite shore. They let go. The barge containing the wagon occupied by Teresa and the sisters began speeding downstream, out of control. The boatman panicked, and Teresa said, "We were all praying; the others were all screaming" (*Foundations*, p. 225).

A local landlord observed the danger of the loose barge and sent some help. Before help arrived, Teresa commented,

> . . . The boatman's son caused in me feelings of great devotion, which I never forget—he must have been ten or eleven years old—for the way he was working so hard upon seeing his father in this difficulty made me praise our Lord. But as His Majesty always gives trials in a compassionate way, so He did here. (*Foundations*, pp. 225–226)

The boat ran into a sandbar and stopped. Help arrived. Teresa and her party were saved.

Teresa ended her account with these words:

> I had not thought of dealing with these things because they are of little importance, and I could have mentioned many bad incidents that occurred on our journeys. But I have been urged to enlarge on my account of this trip. (*Foundations*, p. 226)

Pause: Reflect on the courage you have—or need—to face inner and outer obstacles.

Teresa's Words

This is what I want us to strive for, my Sisters, and let us desire and be occupied in prayer not for the sake of our enjoyment but so as to have this strength to serve. . . . Believe me, Martha and Mary must join together in order to show hospitality to the Lord and have Him always present and not host Him badly by failing to give Him something to eat. How would Mary, always seated at His feet, provide Him with food if her sister did not help her? His food is that in every way possible we draw souls that they may be saved and praise Him always.

You will make two objections: one, that He said that Mary had chosen the better part. The answer is that she had already performed the task of Martha, pleasing the Lord by washing His feet and drying them with her hair. Do you think it would be a small mortification for a woman of nobility like her to wander through these streets (and perhaps alone because her fervent love made her unaware of what she was doing) and enter a house she had never entered before and afterward suffer the criticism of the Pharisee and the very many other things she must have suffered? The people saw a woman like her change so much—and, as we know, she was among such malicious people—and they saw her friendship with the Lord whom they vehemently abhorred, and that she wanted to become a saint since obviously she would have changed her manner of dress and everything else. All of that was enough to cause them comment on the life she had formerly lived. If nowadays there is so much gossip against persons who are not so notorious; what would have been said then? I tell you, Sisters, the better part came after many trials and much mortification, for even if there were no other trial than to see His Majesty abhorred, that would be an intolerable one. Moreover, the many trials that afterward she suffered at the death of the Lord and in the years that she subsequently lived in His absence must have been a terrible torment. You see she wasn't always in the delight of contemplation at the feet of the Lord. (*Interior Castle*, pp. 448–449)

REFLECTION

In counseling her sisters, Teresa told them that they would need courage and determination from beginning to end. Early in the spiritual journey, one needs courage to move beyond a well-ordered, safe life to an authentic engagement in doing the will of God. Later, the virtue of courage enables one to maturely persevere in the face of difficulties.

Courage enters our lives in several ways. Initially, we need courage to overcome our fears and move beyond our pusillanimity. We need courage to endure the ups and downs of life, to develop a balance and stability in the presence of God. Secondly, we need courage to do good in this world—to accomplish a necessary and important task, to continue to live and preach the gospel. Courage overcomes both stagnation and resistance. Throughout our life, the virtue of courage enables us to face sin and respond gratefully to grace.

❧ Meditate with Teresa on the courage of Mary, the woman who anointed the feet of Jesus (John 12:2-8).

❧ Bring to mind someone with whom you need to be reconciled. Imagine a scene in which the two of you meet to talk. In your mind's eye, notice the other person's reactions to you, and reflect on your feelings toward her or him. Now say the words that need to be said to this person in order to mend your relationship. Ponder her or his response to your feelings.

❧ Next, ask yourself, Do I have the courage necessary to be reconciled? Ask God for the strength to act on your desire for reconciliation.

❧ Meditate on Teresa's well-known "bookmark," found in her prayer book:

Let nothing disturb you,
let nothing cause you fear;

All things pass.
God is unchanging.
Patience obtains all:
Whoever has God
needs nothing else.
God alone suffices.

&❧ Recall an event in your life in which you acted with courage. How did this event change the course of your life? Thank God for giving you the courage needed to act bravely.

Where in your life do you most need courage now?

Pray to St. Teresa that you may share in her courageous spirit.

&❧ Dare yourself today to do something that needs to be done. Do it today. Describe the deed in your journal. Call a couple of friends and tell them about what you did. Then spend some time with God conversing about what happened.

GOD'S WORD

One of the Pharisees invited [Jesus] to a meal. When he arrived at the Pharisee's house and took his place at table, suddenly a woman came in, who had a bad name in the town. She had heard he was dining with the Pharisee and had brought with her an alabaster jar of ointment. She waited behind him at his feet, weeping, and her tears fell on his feet, and she wiped them away with her hair; then she covered his feet with kisses and anointed them with the ointment. . . .

Then [Jesus] turned to the woman and said to Simon, "You see this woman? I came into your house, and you poured no water over my feet, but she has poured out her tears over my feet and wiped them away with her hair. You gave me no kiss, but she has been covering my feet with kisses ever since I came in. You did not anoint my head with oil, but she has anointed my feet with ointment. For this reason I tell you that her sins, many as they are, have been forgiven her, because she has shown such great love." (Luke 7:36-38, 44-47)

Closing prayer: Gracious God, give me the courage I need to show my love for you, to overcome my fears and my weakness of soul, and to do the work you have given me to do.

Humility

Theme: God, our Majesty, created us: and God, the Lover, saves us. Realizing, accepting, and thanking God for these two facts is humility—a recognition of our true relationship with God.

Opening prayer: My God, give me humility in regard to myself, in regard to your Majesty, and in regard to your free and multiple gifts. Inscribe this humility in the core of my desiring.

ABOUT TERESA

Teresa told a story about how she began to cultivate the virtue of humility. As a novice, Teresa knew little about how to pray the Office in choir. For a time she neglected learning because she was too involved in other matters. She saw that the other novices could teach her, but she was embarrassed to ask for help: "It occurred to me not to ask them so that they wouldn't find out that I knew so little, and I wouldn't thereby give them bad example" (*Life*, p. 274). Such an attitude, Teresa said, was very common. She learned to recognize it as pride, not humility. As a remedy, she asked the youngest sister for help.

Teresa's growth in humility meant that she became more concerned about truth and less concerned about her image:

I didn't know how to sing well. I was so worried when I hadn't studied what they had entrusted to me . . . that just out of a sheer cult of honor I was so disturbed that I said much less than I knew. I afterward took it upon myself, when I didn't know the assignment very well, simply to say so. I felt this very much in the beginning, but afterward I enjoyed it. And it happened that when I began not to care if they learned I didn't know that I recited much better, and in the effort to get rid of the accursed honor, I came to know how to do what I considered an honor, which, incidentally, each one understands in his own way. (*Life*, pp. 274–275)

Pause: Reflect on humility as the virtue that allows you to accept yourself as you are, the world as it is, and the majesty of God as it is.

TERESA'S WORDS

Teresa wrote a poem that reflected her desire to be what God wanted her to be:

I am Yours and born for You,
What do You want of me?

Majestic Sovereign,
Unending wisdom,
Kindness pleasing to my soul;
God sublime, one Being Good,

Yours, you made me,
Yours, you saved me,
Yours, you endured me,
Yours, you called me,
Yours, you awaited me,
Yours, I did not stray.
What do You want of me?

In Your hand
I place my heart,
Body, life, and soul,
Deep feeling and affections mine,
Spouse—Redeemer sweet,
Myself offered now to you,
What do You want of me?

Give me, if You will, prayer;
Or let me know dryness,
An abundance of devotion,
Or if not, then barrenness.
In you alone, Sovereign Majesty,

I find my peace,
What do You want of me?

Yours I am, for You I was born,
What do You want of me?
(*Poetry*, pp. 377–378)

REFLECTION

Faced with the tremendous mystery of God, Teresa found humility to be the only fitting response. Humility accepts humanity as it is—with its penchants both for good and for ill, with its adequacies and its inadequacies. Humility acknowledges that we do not deserve the gifts of God.

For Teresa, the gift of humility enabled her to speak truthfully of her own "misery," her own need for mercy. With the virtue of humility, she openly and thankfully received the gifts of God, knowing that they were signs of God's love for her. Humility served as the source of her own courage and determination in the movement of reform. Teresa realized that only God's grace allowed her to do what needed to be done.

On a piece of paper, make three columns. In the middle column, outline the qualities you have that make you a gifted human being. In the left-hand column, outline the qualities and faults you had five years ago. In the right-hand column, list the qualities and faults that you may have in another five years, considering what your life is like right now. Bring this bit of your history into prayer, before the throne of God.

❧ Recall a time of humiliation, a point when your pride overreached itself or when you were too stubborn to admit your need for help from God or other people. Bring to mind all of the circumstances leading up to the humiliation. Then think about what happened during and after the humiliating event.

What did you learn from this experience?

How has this humiliation become positive for you?

If it has not, how can you offer it to God and turn it into a moment of gift?

❧ Slow down. Sit quietly. Relax. Breathe deeply and welcome God into your meditation. Imagine a scenario in which you act with ease and confidence. Put yourself in the location and situation. Allow yourself to experience the feelings and the thoughts that are appropriate to the situation. Respond as you wish. Sometime in the next twenty-four hours, act in a social situation the way that you have practiced in your imagination, trusting that God will give you confidence.

❧ Pray the second stanza of Teresa's poem ("Yours, you made me . . ."), repeating the prayer over and over slowly, meditatively. Let the meaning and feelings sink in. On a three-by-five-inch index card, write down the line from the poem that speaks most significantly to you. Use this card as a bookmark in your Bible, and pray the line each time you read the Scriptures.

☙ Read "God's Word" below.
What is the treasure you hold in the earthenware vessel?
Unveil it with a sense of sacred intimacy.

☙ Find the most humble, cherished object in your house. Do something to express your fondness for it.

☙ Reflect on the most "real" person you have known. Compose a prayer of thanks for him or her. Wear something for a day that reminds you of that person.

GOD'S WORD

It is God who said, "Let light shine out of darkness," that has shone into our hearts to enlighten them with the knowledge of God's glory, the glory on the face of Christ. But we hold this treasure in pots of earthen ware, so that the immensity of the power is God's and not our own. We are subjected to every kind of hardship, but never distressed; we see no way out but we never despair; we are pursued but never cut off; knocked down, but still have some life in us; always we carry with us in our body the death of Jesus so that the life of Jesus, too, may be visible in our body. Indeed, while we are still alive, we are continually being handed over to death, for the sake of Jesus, so that the life of Jesus, too, may be visible in our mortal flesh. In us, then, death is at work; in you, life. (2 Corinthians 4:6-12)

Closing prayer: God, in humility, I desire all that you desire for me and all you desire from me.

MEDITATION EIGHT

Obedience

Theme: Obedience is the virtue by which we become reasonable beings capable of free, responsible, and appropriate action in harmony with the will of God.

Opening prayer: "It is no longer I, but Christ living in me" (Galatians 2:20).

ABOUT TERESA

In carrying out her work, Teresa responded sometimes with alacrity, sometimes with hesitation. One instance of her hesitancy appears in her story about founding a new house in Burgos. Due to her fragile health, Teresa actually dreaded going there. She said,

> I couldn't bear the thought of going to a place as cold as Burgos with so many illnesses which would be aggravated by the cold. It would have been rash to make such a long journey just after finishing such a rough one, as I have said, in coming from Soria; nor would Father Provincial allow me to do so. I was reflecting that the prioress of Palencia could easily go, for since everything was in order,

there was now nothing to do. While I was thinking about this and very determined not to go, the Lord spoke to me in the following words in which I saw that the license was already given: "Don't pay attention to the cold weather for I am the true warmth. The devil uses all his strength to hinder that foundation; use yours with my help so that it may be realized and do not fail to go in person, for great good will be done." (*Foundations*, pp. 290–291)

Having heard God speak to her, Teresa changed her mind about going to Burgos. She told God not to take her complaints and fragility seriously because God's help would be enough for any challenge.

Burgos turned out to be as cold and snow-covered as she had feared. But despite her weakened condition and the bad weather, the foundation went smoothly, and she suffered no ill health. God had provided.

Pause: Reflect on what obedience to God means for you.

TERESA'S WORDS

What I intend to explain is why obedience, in my opinion, is the quickest or best means for reaching this most happy state. The reason is that since we are by no means lords of our own will in such a way that we can employ it purely and simply in God, obedience is the true path for subjecting it to reason. For this subjection is not accomplished by means of good reasons; human nature and self-love can find so many of them that we would never arrive at the goal. And often the most reasonable thing seems to us foolish if it is not to our advantage.

Well, what is the remedy? That in obedience, just as in a very dubious litigation, a judge is accepted and both sides place the matter is his hands. Tired of arguing, our soul accepts one who may be either the superior or the confessor with the determination not to have any more argument or to think any more of its own case but to trust the words of the Lord who says, *Whoever hears you hears Me,* and it disregards its own will. The Lord esteems this surrender very much, and rightly so, because it means making Him Lord over the free will He has given us. By exercising ourselves in this surrender, sometimes denying ourselves, at other times waging a thousand battles since the judgment made in our case seems to us absurd, we come to be conformed with what they command us. It can be a painful exercise, but with or without the pain we in the end do what is commanded, and the Lord helps so much on His part that for the same reason that we subject our will and reason to Him He makes us lords over our own will. Then, beings lords of ourselves, we can with perfection be occupied with God, giving Him a pure will that He may join it with His, asking Him to send fire from heaven so that His love may burn this sacrifice and take away everything that could displease Him. We have done what we can by placing the sacrifice on the altar, although through much hardship. And, insofar as is in our power, the sacrifice remains on the altar and does not touch the ground. (*Foundations*, pp. 120–121)

REFLECTION

Teresa often spoke about obedience to her superiors, her confessors, and her sisters. The purpose of obedience is to unite a person's will—weak and vacillating, or strong and tyrannical— with the will of God.

The practice of obedience covers a spectrum: a person's desires are sometimes tempered, sometimes enkindled. On some occasions, the soul is challenged to complete tasks seemingly beyond itself; on other occasions, the soul is challenged to maintain a life of balance and moderation.

Although *obedience* is a rather suspect word in our culture, most of us consult, and like to consult, with other people about our choices, our situations, our feelings, and our actions— within joyful or sorrowful circumstances. We know that the understanding ear and the discriminating directive of another person stabilizes us, enables us to move forward productively, and makes a place for us within a larger world. This trust in another person, within the right context, can unite us in and with the mystery of God.

Teresa, also, was faithful and obedient to her own conscience and to the inner words she had learned to recognize as being from God. The exercise of obedience made her a partner in the works of God, which time itself ratified.

☙ Meditatively read "Teresa's Words" again. Spend time listening to Teresa speak these words to you. When you come across a passage that is especially enlightening or perplexing, talk about the passage with Teresa. Ask her and ask yourself what the passage means. Talk about why you find it illuminating or challenging. When you have concluded your dialog, write down some or your reflections about "Teresa's Words."

☙ Recall times when you have disclosed important matters of your heart and soul to someone who was competent to listen to and understand you. Close your eyes; focus on one of these important times of self-disclosure. Who was the other person? What did you disclose? By reflecting on the following questions, let all the feelings of that moment recur now:

Why was your revelation to the other person so important?

How did you benefit from their listening and advice?

Are you a better person because of that discussion?

How did God touch you in the disclosure?

How was the discussion part of your being obedient to God's plan for you?

❧ With a pencil and a sheet of paper, draw an image of what the word *obedience* awakens in you. In the presence of God, attempt to discern how this image relates to the obedience in faith owed to God alone.

Sometimes the most difficult aspect of being obedient to God's will is discerning what God's will is. We certainly have many sources of help: the Scriptures, confidants, our consciences, tradition, reason, our hearts, and most essentially, God's whispered word in all of our lives.

Bring to mind an issue or decision that presently vexes you. Remembering God's constant, loving presence, bring this issue or decision to God. The following outline may facilitate your discussion with God:

1. *Open the discussion by praying*: "Gracious God, I desire to do your will in all things. Lead me to understand your will and to obey it wholeheartedly."
2. *Ponder the issue or decision*: Describe all sides or aspects of the issue to God. Ask yourself these questions:
   What are the values involved?
   What are my feelings (be sure to spend time exploring all your feelings)?

Who is involved?

What actions would be required of me?

What are good reasons for each course of action?

3. *Examine your intentions:* What effects do I want my decision to have? Am I being driven by any prejudices or irrational motives?

4. *Reflect on God's word in the Scriptures:* Are there any stories or teachings in the Scriptures that throw light on this issue?

5. *Ponder the Great Commandments*: What do the love of God and love of neighbor ask of me?

6. *Seek advice*: Disclosing your problem to a wise and helpful friend is prayer too. Another source of advice is Christian tradition: does it shed light on your situation?

7. *Pray again:* Listen to the voice of God deep within your soul.

8. *Make your decision and act on it:* Pray always that God's will is done.

❧ Reflect on any of the "addiction" issues of today (for example, drug or alcohol abuse, perfectionism, relational tyranny, or eating disorders). Are you called in any way to enable other people who are victimized by one of these addictions to become "masters of their own will"? Reflect on the talents God has given you to help other people liberate themselves.

❧ In what relationship in your life do you find it most difficult to be reasonable? Ask God for the spirit of peace.

❧ In what relationship in your life do you find it most difficult to be spontaneous? Ask God for the spirit of freedom.

GOD'S WORD

Ahab called all Israel together and assembled the prophets on Mount Carmel. Elijah stepped out in front of all the people. "How long," he said, "do you mean to hobble first on one leg then on the other? If Yahweh is God, follow him; if Baal, follow him." But the people had nothing to say. Elijah then said to them, "I, I alone, am left as a prophet of Yahweh, while the prophets of Baal are four hundred and fifty. Let two bulls be given us; let them choose one for themselves, dismember it but not set fire to it. I in my turn shall prepare the other bull, but not set fire to it. You must call on the name of your god, and I shall call on the name of Yahweh; the god who answers with fire, is God indeed." The people all answered, "Agreed!"

At the time when the offering is presented, Elijah the prophet stepped forward. "Yahweh, God of Abraham, Isaac and Israel," he said, "let them know today that you are God in Israel, and that I am your servant, that I have done all these things at your command. Answer me, Yahweh, answer me, so that this people may know that you, Yahweh, are God and are winning back their hearts."

Then Yahweh's fire fell and consumed the burnt offering and the wood and licked up the water in the trench. When all the people saw this they fell on their faces. "Yahweh is God," they cried, "Yahweh is God!" (1 Kings 18:20-24, 36-39)

Closing prayer: "May You through Your providence, Lord, provide the necessary means by which my soul may serve You at Your pleasure rather than at its own. . . . May this 'I' die, and may another live in me greater than I and better for me than I, so that I may serve Him" (Teresa, *Soliloquies,* in *The Collected Works of St. Teresa of Ávila,* vol. 1, p. 462).

MEDITATION NINE

Simplicity of Life

Theme: Simplicity in communal life includes work that enables contemplation but provides for the necessities of life.

Opening prayer: God, open my mind and my heart to reflect on the work that I do to provide for the necessities of life. Give me a discerning spirit that sees all things in relation to you.

ABOUT TERESA

In founding new houses, Teresa resisted putting them under people's patronage and financial commitment, which she called "having income." She desired that the new houses be self-supporting, according to the economics of the time, and that they be somewhat dependent on the generosity of the local civic community. In *The Constitutions*, Teresa describes the simplicity of life that she desired for her sisters:

Let them live always on alms and without any income, but insofar as possible let there be no begging. Great must be the need that makes them resort to begging. Rather, they should help themselves with the work of their hands, as St. Paul did; the Lord will provide what they need. Provided they want no more than this and are content to live simply, they will have what is necessary to sustain life. If they strive with all their might to please the Lord, His Majesty will keep them from want. Their earnings must not come from work requiring careful attention to fine details but from spinning and sewing or other unrefined labor that does not so occupy the mind as to keep it from the Lord. Nor should they do work with gold or silver. Neither should there be any haggling over what is offered for their work. They should graciously accept what is given. If they see that the amount offered is insufficient, they should not take on the work. (*The Collected Works of St. Teresa of Ávila,* vol. 3, p. 321)

Pause: Ponder the relationship between spiritual poverty or simplicity and your own financial situation.

TERESA'S WORDS

Believe me, my daughters, that for your good the Lord has given me a little understanding of the blessings that lie in holy poverty. Those who experience them will understand, though perhaps not as much as I. For not only had I failed to be poor in spirit, even though I professed it, but I was foolish in spirit. Poverty of spirit is a good that includes within itself all the good things of the world. . . . In it lies great dominion. I say that it gives once again to one who doesn't care about the world's good things dominion over them all. What do kings and lords matter to me if I don't want their riches, or don't care to please them if in order to do so I would have to displease God in even the smallest thing? Nor what do I care about their honors if I have understood that the greatest honor of a poor person lies in the fact of his being truly poor?

In my opinion honor and money almost always go together; anyone who wants honor doesn't despise money, and anyone who despises money doesn't care much about honor. Let this be clearly understood, for it seems to me that the desire for honor always brings with it some interest in money or income. It would be a wonder if any poor person were honored in the world; on the contrary, even though he may be worthy of honor, he is little esteemed. True poverty brings with it overwhelming honor. Poverty that is chosen for God alone has no need of pleasing anyone but Him. It is certain that in having need of no one a person has many friends. I have become clearly aware of this through experience. (*The Way of Perfection*, in *The Collected Works of St. Teresa of Ávila*, vol. 2, p. 45)

REFLECTION

When Teresa spoke of founding her houses "in poverty," she meant self-support by marketable work. She wanted neither begging nor income assured by patronage. In taking this stance, Teresa considered several factors: the type of work that allowed the sisters to maintain an atmosphere of prayer, a style of life that was satisfied with necessities, and a communal independence that was maintained by the sisters' daily work and by civic almsgiving.

In our day and age, according to our responsibilities in life, we are continually called upon to reflect on our work, our economic resources, our lifestyle, and our role in the general economy of our city, nation, and world. Teresa, from her day and age, gives us several ways to think about income-producing work and living simply.

❧ Read "Teresa's Words" at least one more time. Pick out one passage that strikes you as especially important. Spend time with this passage; let its meaning touch you.

❧ Pose these questions, in which *our* refers to your family, or your community, or your colleagues at work:

How does our work relate to our ongoing dialog with God?

What is our work atmosphere?

How do we exercise our responsibilities for providing what is necessary to support ourselves and those who are dependent on us?

How does our type of work affect our value system?

Are we taken with luxuries?

❧ Pray about your work. Talk with God about how your work relates to your life with God and how it impacts the simplicity or lack of it in your lifestyle.

❧ Reflect on this saying of Teresa: "Poverty that is chosen for God alone has no need of pleasing anyone but Him. It is certain that in having need of no one a person has many friends. I have become clearly aware of this through experience" (*Way of Perfection*, p. 45).

Can you think of any instances in your own experience that support Teresa's notion of poverty?

❧ Poverty, in Teresa's sense, had to do with her community being as independent as possible from the influence and ethos of wealthy persons. She did not want her sisters to be dependent on anyone for their livelihood. Rather, she wanted them to work and to rely on the gifts that God gave them. Does this sense of Christian poverty appeal to you? Why or why not?

❧ To ensure an atmosphere of quiet reflection, Teresa wrote in *The Constitutions*, "Let there never be a common workroom" (p. 321). Reflect on the difference between projects worked on in uninterrupted privacy and projects done with or in the presence of other people. Thank God for the freedom and the creativity found in each.

❧ Write down a few economic surprises, positive or negative, that have been a part of your life. What did they teach you about the reality of this world? About the reality of God?

GOD'S WORD

I have never asked anyone for money or clothes; you know for yourselves that these hands of mine earned enough to meet my needs and those of my companions. By every means I have shown you that we must exert ourselves in this way to support the weak, remembering the words of the Lord Jesus who himself said, "There is more happiness in giving than in receiving." (Acts 20:33-35)

Closing prayer: Convert our hearts to you, O God, that we may be mindful of all your gifts. Keep us free in our work and just in our exchanges. Give us simplicity of life and poverty of spirit.

MEDITATION TEN
Friendship with Christ

Theme: As persons of prayer, we are called to share with Christ the joys and sorrows that any intimate friendship entails.

Opening prayer:

Myself surrendered and given,
The exchange is this:
My Beloved is for me,
And I am for my Beloved.
(Teresa, *Poetry*, p. 379)

ABOUT TERESA

Teresa compared growth in a relationship with God to the processes of acquaintance, friendship, engagement, and marriage. She said that when a woman and a man become engaged, they talk about their similarities and differences, and their love for one another; and they try to spend as much time as possible together. Friendship with God is similar. Teresa told her sisters,

So, too, in the case of this union with God, the agreement has been made, and this soul is well informed about the goodness of her Spouse and determined to do His will in everything and in as many ways as she sees might make Him happy. And His Majesty, as one who understands clearly whether these things about his betrothed are so, is happy with her. As a result He grants this mercy, for He desired her to know Him more and that they might meet together, as they say, and be united. (*Interior Castle*, p. 355)

Pause: Reflect on what "engagement with God" means to you.

TERESA'S WORDS

Having spoken one day to a person who had given up a great deal for God and recalling how I had never given up anything for Him—nor have I served Him in accordance with my obligation—and considering the many favors he had bestowed on my soul, I began to grow very anxious. And the Lord said: "You already know of the espousal between you and Me. Because of this espousal, whatever I have is yours. So I give you all the trials and sufferings I underwent, and by these means, as with something belonging to you, you can make requests of my Father." Although I had heard we share these, now I had heard it in such a different way that it seemed I felt great dominion. The friendship in which this favor was granted me cannot be described here. It seemed to me the Father accepted the fact of this sharing; and since then I look very differently upon what the Lord suffered, as something belonging to me—and it gives me great comfort. (*Spiritual Testimonies*, p. 412)

REFLECTION

In Teresa's depiction of the mystical life, she speaks of union with God in love as the culmination of the mystery of faith. One enters into the seventh dwelling, the center of one's own soul, where God dwells. In the fifth dwelling, she speaks of being "betrothed to," or engaged with, God.

Teresa's life of prayer engaged her more closely to God, and this engagement affected her life projects, her consolations and desolations, and her successes and difficulties. In every respect, Teresa believed that this spiritual betrothal was a reciprocal exchange and a mutual commitment in a shared life and love.

The period before marriage that we call "engagement" is marked by not-yet-perfected, not-yet-secured, not-yet-finalized commitment and involvement. The engaged couple discover their similarities and differences, and they maintain more relationships than marriage will allow time for. There are normally moments of unsought grace and inevitable shortcomings. Despite its hazards and unique pains, this period in a relationship invigorates, challenges, and opens the couple to the expanse and grandeur of life. By analogy, Teresa realized that our engagement and intimacy with God is a profound experience of life, challenge, and expansion for us.

☙ Chart some of the ups and downs of your friendship, or engagement, with Christ. Consider making a progress chart that allows you to plot these ups and downs. Write a brief description of each high and low point.

This guided meditation may assist you to engage yourself with Jesus:

Begin by relaxing each part of your body, starting with your feet and ending with your face. . . . Flex and relax each part of your body. . . . Then close your eyes and focus on deep breathing. . . . Breathe slowly and calmly, letting life fill your body. . . .

You are in a forest clearing, waiting for Jesus. . . . The giant oak trees rustle with the warm breeze. . . . You take a seat on a bench. . . . Cardinals and mockingbirds flit in and out of the shadows. . . . Far overhead, a hawk floats on the currents. . . . Wildflowers in yellows and violets wave along a path. . . .

As you look down the path, you see Jesus walking slowly toward you. . . . You stand up to greet him. . . . Grateful for his coming and knowing of his love, you embrace him. . . . Jesus says, "My friend. . . ."

As the two of you sit down together, Jesus asks you to speak about your feelings for him, your hopes and fears for the relationship. . . . Knowing that he loves you completely, you begin to pour out your thoughts and feelings. . . .

When you have finished talking, he says, "Know that I will always be with you, and that I love you eternally. Be at peace about us, as long as we can talk and be honest. Now I am going, but my spirit will always be with you." . . .

When you have completed your guided meditation, you may want to write down any reflections about it and about your relationship with Jesus.

❧ Pray Jesus' words "Remain in me" repeatedly.

❧ Recall the first weeks or months of an important friendship. Spend time making a collage that represents the ups and downs, the variety of emotions, and the important events of the friendship. Pray for your friend, and share your collage with someone when you finish it.

GOD'S WORD

This is my commandment:
love one another,
as I have loved you.
No one can have greater love
than to lay down his life for his friends.
You are my friends,
if you do what I command you.
I shall no longer call you servants,

because a servant does not know
the master's business;
I call you friends,
because I have made known to you
everything I have learned from my Father.
(John 15:12-15)

Closing prayer: "Your Father gave You to us, may I not lose, my Lord, so precious a jewel" (Teresa, *Soliloquies*, p. 458).

Attending to the Word of God

Theme: God speaks to us in many modes. Teresa described three ways of knowing the authentic word of God.

Opening prayer: "O Lord, my God, how You possess the words of eternal life, where all mortals will find what they desire if they want to seek it!. . . . You are almighty; Your works are incomprehensible. Bring it about, then, Lord, that my thoughts not withdraw from Your words" (Teresa, *Soliloquies*, p. 450).

ABOUT TERESA

Almost nonchalantly, Teresa wrote about God speaking to her. Whether God's word was consoling or commanding, Teresa attended to it:

One day, while I was in prayer beseeching our Lord to give [the Carmelite nuns] a house since they were His brides and had such desire to please Him, He told me: "I have already heard you; leave it to Me." I was left feeling very happy since it seemed I already had the house. And this was so. His Majesty prevented us from buying one that because of its nice location was pleasing to all. But the house itself was so old and run down that only the site was being bought and for not much less than was paid for the house we have now. Though all was agreed upon and only the contract remained to be drawn up, I was by no means satisfied. This didn't seem to be in accord with the words I had heard in prayer; for those words, I believed, were a sign that a good house would be given to us. And thus the Lord was pleased that the owner, even though he was making a great profit, should raise a difficulty about signing the contract at the established time, and we were able, without any fault, to get out of the agreement. (*Foundations*, p. 231)

Teresa considered this move an act of the providence of God, who proves true to the given word.

Pause: Reflect on the comfort and the challenge that the word of God has brought to you.

Teresa's Words

Teresa describes three signs that indicate if the words heard, either from outside ourselves or from within ourselves, are the words of God:

The surest signs they are from God that can be had, in my opinion, are these: The first and truest is the power and authority they bear, for locutions from God effect what they say. Let me explain myself better. A soul finds itself in the midst of all the tribulation and disturbance that was mentioned, in darkness of the intellect and in dryness; with one word alone of these locutions from the Lord ("don't be distressed"), it is left calm and free from all distress, with great light, and without all that suffering in which it seemed to it that all the learned men and all who might come together to give it reasons for not being distressed would be unable to remove its affliction no matter how hard they tried. Or, it is afflicted because its confessor and others have told it that its spirit is from the devil, and it is all full of fear; with one word alone ("It is I, fear not"), the fear is taken away completely, and the soul is most comforted, thinking that nothing would be sufficient to make it believe anything else. Or, it is greatly distressed over how certain serious business matters will turn out; it hears that it should be calm, that everything will turn out all right. It is left certain and free of anxiety. And this is the way in many other instances.

The second sign is the great quiet left in the soul, the devout and peaceful recollection, the readiness to engage in the praises of God. . . .

The third sign is that these words remain in the memory for a very long time, and some are never forgotten, as are those we listen to here on earth—I mean those we hear from men. For even if the words are spoken by men who are very important and learned, or concern the future, we do not have them engraved on our memory, or believe them, as we do these. The certitude is so strong that even in things that in one's own opinion sometimes seem impossible and in which there is doubt as to whether they will to will not happen, and the intellect wavers, there is an assurance in the soul itself that cannot be overcome. Even though it seems that everything is going contrary to what the soul understood, and years go by, the thought remains that God will find other means than those men know of and that in the end the words will be accomplished; and so they are. (*Interior Castle*, pp. 372–373)

REFLECTION

For Teresa and for us, the modes of hearing the word of God are varied, but the effectiveness of the word in our minds and hearts is the same. Word and Spirit act together. God's word carries power and authority. The quick-coming peace or joy from God's word is always a wondrous surprise, and the word of God resides in our memory as long as we live. Teresa's astute depiction of this threefold activity of God's word and her commitment to live by this word earned her the title "doctor of the church."

❧ Recalling the three signs of the authentic word of God can prove to be beneficial as we reflect on our experiences and as we try to discern God's will for us. Sometimes the Spirit moves us quickly from anxiety to calm, bringing a deeper level of surety and a readiness to express our gratitude. Other movements leave us intuitively confident about a fulfilling future. These movements of God's Spirit in us awaken trust, a sense of promise, and an attentiveness to the gradual unfolding of time.

❧ Meditatively read the story in "About Teresa" again. Then reflect on your own life.

Has God acted in your life in a similar way?

Do you see any signs that God has spoken to you through broken deals, disappointments, or surprises?

Think of one incident that seemed at the time, or still seems, devoid of explanation but which turned out well for you in the long run.

Now apply Teresa's threefold test to see if, indeed, God was telling you something:

Did the "right thing," or intuition, to act or not act come powerfully?

Did the decision or action calm your spirit?

Has the decision or action stayed in your memory as a moment of illumination or goodness?

If you keep a journal, you might want to write your responses to these questions now, and then come back in some days or weeks and reconsider your responses. God does still speak in history, but we may not hear God clearly until some time later.

🍃 Reflect on an instance when you heard the word of God in the form of promise. Write about two moments—the moment when you sensed the promise, and the moment when the promise proved true. Spend some time talking with God about this promise.

🍃 Recall an instance when the word of God came to you from a voice outside yourself. Relive the situation in your imagination: remember the circumstances, sense the environment, hear the voice, recall the message, and reawaken the resonance of your own heart.

🍃 Pray for the prophetic spirit in the church.

🍃 Go for a walk in the early morning or evening and listen closely to all the sounds in the air. Sing, hum, or whistle a song of praise and thanks, or maybe dance to a song of praise.

🍃 After reading "God's Word," meditate on Mary, who heard the word of God and kept it.

GOD'S WORD

In the sixth month the angel Gabriel was sent by God to a town in Galilee called Nazareth, to a virgin betrothed to a man named Joseph, of the House of David; and the virgin's name was Mary. He went in and said to her, "Rejoice, you who enjoy God's favor. The Lord is with you." She was deeply disturbed by these words and asked herself what this greeting could mean, but the angel said to her, "Mary, do not be afraid; you have won God's favor. Look! You are to conceive in your womb and bear a son, and you must name him Jesus. He will be great and will be called Son of the Most High. . . . God will give him the throne of his ancestor David; he will rule over the House of Jacob for ever and his reign will have no end." Mary said to the angel, "But how can this come about, since I have no knowledge of man?" The angel answered, "The Holy Spirit will come upon you, and the power of the Most High will cover you with its shadow. And so the child will be holy and will be called Son of God. And I tell you this too: your cousin Elizabeth also, in her old age, has conceived a son, and she whom people called barren is now in her sixth month, for nothing is impossible to God." Mary said, "You see before you the Lord's servant, let it happen to me as you have said." And the angel left her.

Mary set out at that time and went as quickly as she could into the hill country to a town in Judah. She went into Zechariah's house and greeted Elizabeth. Now it happened that as soon as Elizabeth heard Mary's greeting, the child leapt in her womb and Elizabeth was filled with the Holy Spirit. She gave a loud cry and said, "Of all women you are the most blessed, and blessed is the fruit of your womb. Why should I be honored with a visit from the mother of my Lord? Look, the moment your greeting reached my ears, the child in my womb leapt for joy. Yes, blessed is she who believed that the promise made her by the Lord would be fulfilled." (Luke 1:26-45)

Closing prayer: O You, who speak to us in so many ways, may your word make its home in my heart, abide in me all my days, and be born into the world in my deeds.

MEDITATION TWELVE

Envisioning the Mysteries of God

Theme: Envisioning the mysteries of God means becoming aware of, through the action of the Spirit, how true they are.

Opening prayer: God of light and darkness, if you find me ready, open the eyes of my mind to see your glory.

ABOUT TERESA

Teresa knew the truths of faith—the teachings of the church. But she said that as she continued to pray, in a surprising and wonderful way, she began to see how "true" these truths really were. But she was hard-pressed to explain how this revelation happened.

> I have been wanting to find some comparison by which to explain what I'm speaking about, and I don't think there is any that fits. But let's use this one; you enter into the room of a king or great lord, or I believe they call it the treasure chamber, where there are countless kinds of glass and earthen vessels and other things so arranged that almost all

these objects are seen upon entering. Once I was brought to a room like this in the house of the Duchess of Alba where, while I was on a journey, obedience ordered me to stay because of this lady's insistence with my superiors. I was amazed on entering and wondered what benefit could be gained from that conglomeration of things, and I saw that one could praise the Lord at seeing so many different kinds of objects, and now I laugh to myself upon realizing how the experience has helped me here in my explanation. Although I was in that room for a while, there was so much there to see that I soon forgot it all; none of those pieces has remained in my memory any more than if I had never seen them, nor would I know how to explain the workmanship of any of them. I can only say in general that I remember seeing everything. Likewise with this favor, the soul, while it is made one with God, is placed in this room of the empyreal heaven that we must have interiorly. (*Interior Castle*, pp. 381–382)

Pause: Reflect on what "seeing" the truths of faith means to you.

TERESA'S WORDS

It could be that some of you do not know what a vision is, especially an intellectual one. . . . Oh, daughters, they are so great one cannot exaggerate! For even through they are unexplainable, they are well inscribed in the very interior part of the soul and are never forgotten.

But, you will insist, if there is no image and the faculties do not understand, how can the visions be remembered? I don't understand this either; but I do understand that some truths about the grandeur of God remain so fixed in this soul, that even if faith were not to tell it who God is and of its obligation to believe that He is God, from that very moment it would adore Him as God, as did Jacob when he saw the ladder. By means of the ladder Jacob must have understood other secrets that he didn't know how to explain, for by seeing just a ladder on which angels descended and ascended he would not have understood such great mysteries if there had not been deeper interior enlightenment. I don't know if I'm guessing right in what I say, for although I have heard this story about Jacob, I don't know if I am remembering it correctly. (*Interior Castle*, pp. 380–381)

REFLECTION

As Teresa grew in a life of prayer, she began to be aware of the difference between her role and God's role during prayer. As Teresa better understood the graces of prayer, she spoke of visions, raptures, and locutions.

Because Teresa wrote to explain herself, to help her sisters understand prayer, and to encourage them in this sometimes difficult task, she defined what she meant by intellectual visions: In these visions, one understands the hidden things of God with surety and clarity. Although intellectual visions cannot be described, they are never forgotten.

Intellectual visions give one a sense of the magnificence of the mystery of God. An intellectual vision of divine things is a self-authenticating experience: you know, and you are intellectually aware that you know, the truths of faith. This visionary experience gives both love and clarity to the things of God.

☙ Have your ever had an experience that revealed the wonder of God? Search your memory for a time when you knew the magnificence of the mystery of God. Ponder your memory of this moment, its enduring effects, and the grounding in hope it has given you. Praise and thank God for this experience.

☙ Find passages in Scripture that speak of visions you do not understand: for example, Ezekiel's wheels among wheels (Ezekiel 1:4-28), the horses of the apocalypse (Revelation 6), Jesus' walking on water (Matthew 14:22-33), or the creation of Eve and Adam (Genesis 1:26—2). Read each passage carefully. Meditate on the mystery of God revealed in each passage. Be aware of both the darkness and the light of your mind in approaching these passages. Converse with God about each one.

❧ Try to list six meanings for the phrase, "to see God." Then find four friends and ask them what the phrase means to them. Pray for the Spirit's gift of knowledge to be given to you and to other people who need it. If you find yourself in a period of darkness, pray repeatedly, in harmony with your breathing, "Come, Light."

❧ Pray for those who find themselves blind in their faith. Offer their names and situations to the Holy Spirit.

❧ Go out on a sunny day with your sunglasses on. Take them off. Squint. Thank God for the light of the sun. Put the sunglasses back on. Be content.

GOD'S WORD

Jacob left Beersheba and set out for Haran. When he had reached a certain place, he stopped there for the night, since the sun had set. Taking one of the stones of that place, he made it his pillow and lay down where he was. He had a dream: there was a ladder, planted on the ground with its top reaching to heaven; and God's angels were going up and down on it. . . . Then Jacob awoke from his sleep and said, "Truly, Yahweh is in this place and I did not know!" He was afraid and said, "How awe inspiring this place is! This is nothing less than the abode of God, and this is the gate of heaven!" Early [the] next morning, Jacob took the stone he had used for his pillow, and set it up as a pillar, pouring oil over the top of it. He named the place Bethel, but before that the town had been called Luz. (Genesis 28:10-12, 16-19)

Closing prayer: "O Lord, my God! I weep for the time I didn't understand; and since You know, my God, the great number who don't want to understand, I now beg You, Lord, let there be at least one, at least one who will see Your light so that many might possess it" (Teresa, *Soliloquies*, p. 454).

MEDITATION THIRTEEN

Spiritual Pain

Theme: On the spiritual journey, we will probably, sooner or later, experience what Teresa called "spiritual pain."

Opening prayer:

Lord, end now
This long agony.
Comfort your servant
Sighing for You.
Shatter the fetters
Let her rejoice.
Longing to see You,
Death I desire.
(Teresa, *Poetry*, p. 384)

ABOUT TERESA

In her own life, Teresa suffered physically. She was ill quite regularly from 1539 to 1542. Teresa also had to cope with emotional difficulties; for instance, her mother died when Teresa was thirteen years old.

Throughout Teresa's adulthood, chronic illness and social misunderstandings were part of her life. She alluded to these sufferings and struggles, but she did not highlight them. During the time of the foundations, Teresa met up with slander, calumny, and gross opposition. Loneliness, anxiety, fear, and desolation were no strangers to her either.

Teresa recorded that her courage failed her on November 8, 1575 in Seville. An overwhelming conviction of her own sinfulness coupled with a fear of persecution stunned her and sapped her usually vigorous spirit. Even reasoning that these trials would be good for her did not dispel the gloom from Teresa's soul. She wrote:

The fear didn't go away, and what I felt was a vexing war. I chanced upon a letter in which my good Father [Gratian] refers to what St. Paul says, that God does not permit us to be tempted beyond what we can suffer. That comforted me a lot, but it wasn't enough. Rather, the next day I became sorely afflicted in seeing I was without him, since I had no one to whom I could have recourse in this tribulation. It seemed to me I was living in great loneliness, and this loneliness increased when I saw there was no one now but him who might give me comfort and that he had to be absent most of the time, which was a great torment to me. (*Spiritual Testimonies*, p. 415)

Pause: Reflect on the spiritual pain in your life.

TERESA'S WORDS

For in this state [of spiritual pain] grace is so hidden . . . that not even a very tiny spark is visible. The soul doesn't think that it has any love of God or that it ever had any, for it has done some good, or His Majesty has granted it some favor, all of this seems to have been dreamed up or fancied. As for sins, it sees certainly that it has committed them.

O Jesus, and what a thing it is to see this kind of forsaken soul; and, as I have said, what little help any earthly consolation is for it! Hence, do not think, Sisters, if at some time you find yourselves in this state, that the rich and those who are free will have a better remedy for these times of suffering. Absolutely not, for being rich in this case seems to me like the situation of a person condemned to die who has all the world's delights placed before him. These delights would not be sufficient to alleviate his suffering; rather, they would increase the torment. So it is with this torment; it comes from above, and earthly things are of no avail in this matter. Our great God wants us to know our own misery and that He is king; and this is very important for what lies ahead. . . .

Is it true that [the soul] will know how to explain its experiences? They are indescribable, for they are spiritual afflictions and sufferings that one cannot name. The best remedy (I don't mean for getting rid of them, because I don't find any, but so that they may be endured) is to engage in external works of charity and to hope in the mercy of God who never fails those who hope in Him. May He be forever blessed, amen. (*Interior Castle*, pp. 364–365)

REFLECTION

Our time is certainly different from Teresa's time. We have the health sciences, psychology, social analysis, and even economics to help us uncover our difficulties and direct us toward health. These aids should not be discounted.

And yet, some dimensions of life seem to resist resolution, even with the insights and methods that come from these fields. The restless search for a life of value may reveal to us a seeming void in our life. As we mature, a harder pain, a more total searing seems to happen within us. Upon examination, this pain may not be linked to knowable causes alone, and so the remedy for the pain escapes us and remains inaccessible.

Thanks to Teresa's writings, we know that such spiritual pain can exist. We may find this pain in ourselves; we may find it in others who come to us to speak about their life and the meaning of their life in the presence of ultimate mystery. Ultimate mystery is the nature of God.

❧ Read "About Teresa" again—slowly and carefully, noting her description of spiritual pain. Then recall the most painful experience of your life. Using art materials (e.g., clay, paints, or markers), depict this experience in design and color. Or write, as clearly and thoroughly as possible, a description of the event and your desolation.

❧ Next, meditate on "Teresa's Words." When you have finished, ponder and pray over these questions:

Am I satisfied that some spiritual pain is mysterious and that the causes of it are often impossible to detect?

Have I sought remedy for my difficulties in "earthly consolation" when I knew that only hope in God could really provide consolation?

Can I engage in "external works of charity" while enduring spiritual pain?

❧ Ponder, open-eyed, some horrific event—for instance, the evil of the Holocaust or the pains of a cancer victim. To learn of the latest disaster, just open your newspaper; plenty of horrific events are recorded each day. Contemplate the event, seeking the pain but not "resolving" it. In prayer or through some ritual action, honor the suffering of the person or people involved.

🙚 Read and talk with God about Galatians 2:20-21. Contemplate a crucifix. Ask yourself, Who is this nailed here? Jesus? Yourself? Your neighbor?

Reflect on what this "promise" of God's means to you: "This comes from God, for you have been granted the privilege for Christ's sake not only of believing in him but of suffering for him as well" (Philippians 1:29).

🙚 Go to a nearby church or chapel and make the Stations of the Cross.

🙚 Read "God's Word." Then, keeping clearly in mind each aspect of the crucifixion of Jesus, imagine yourself at the foot of the cross—seeing, hearing, smelling, touching, all that is there. Enter into the scene fully. When you are present at the cross, pray the Jesus Prayer out loud: "Lord Jesus Christ, have mercy on me, a sinner."

GOD'S WORD

The passers-by jeered at him; they shook their heads and said, "Aha! So you would destroy the Temple and rebuild it in three days! Then save yourself; come down from the cross!" The chief priests and the scribes mocked him among themselves in the same way with the words, "He saved others, he cannot save himself. Let the Christ, the king of Israel, come down from the cross now, for us to see it and believe!" Even those who were crucified with him taunted him.

When the sixth hour came there was darkness over the whole land until the ninth hour. And at the ninth hour Jesus cried out in a loud voice, "Eloi, eloi, lama sabachthani?" which means, "My God, my God, why have you forsaken me?" When some of those who stood by heard this, they said, "Listen, he is calling on Elijah." Someone ran and soaked a sponge in vinegar and, putting it on a reed, gave it to him to drink saying, "Wait! And see if Elijah will come to take him down." But Jesus gave a loud cry and breathed his last. And the veil of the Sanctuary was torn in two from top to bottom. (Mark 15:29-38)

Closing prayer: In my pain, O God, enable me to bring myself into the passion and death of your son so that I may, in the Spirit, be brought to the resurrection.

Meditation Fourteen

Love

Theme: Love is from God. Perfect love is possible only between two people who both love God.

Opening prayer: God, who is love, give us yourself. Teach us to love.

About Teresa

Teresa often alludes to both men and women friends she knew and loved. Appreciation for the charity and affection she was shown runs deeply in her correspondence. For instance, in one of her letters, Teresa describes the generosity of Doña María de Mendoza, the sister of one of Teresa's supporters—the bishop of Ávila.

On August 15, 1568, Teresa and her sisters moved into a new monastery. Almost immediately they all became ill. Doña María, who already had the reputation for being generous to poor people, came to the community's aid:

When [María] saw the situation, and before I spoke to her about the matter, she showed me much charity. . . . [She] saw that we could not remain there without great hardship and also that the site was far from where we could receive alms, as well as unhealthy, she told us to give that house to her and that she would buy us another. And this she did. The one she gave us was worth much more, and in addition she has given all that is necessary up till now, and she will do so as long as she lives. (*Foundations*, p. 147)

Pause: Reflect on one person in your life whom you especially appreciate and love.

TERESA'S WORDS

Teresa composed discourses on love and friendship, and defended the love of those who love God:

It will seem to you that [spiritual] persons do not love or know anyone but God. I say, yes they do love, with a much greater and more genuine love, and with passion, and with a more beneficial love; in short, it is love. And these souls are more inclined to give than to receive. Even with respect to the Creator Himself they want to give more than to receive. I say that this attitude is what merits the name "love." . . .

As soon as these persons love, they go beyond the bodies and turn their eyes to the soul and look to see if there is something to love in the soul. And if there isn't anything lovable, but they see some beginning and readiness so that if they love this soul and dig in this mine they will find gold, their labor causes them no pain. Nothing could be presented to them that they wouldn't eagerly do for the good of this soul, for they desire to continue loving it; but they know that if it does not love God very much and have His blessings, their loving it is impossible. And I say that this is impossible, no matter how much they are obligated to it; and even if it dies with love for them and does all the good works it can for them and possesses all natural graces combined, their wills will not have the strength to love it or make this love last. . . . For it is a love that must end when they die if the other is not keeping the law of God, and these persons understand that the other does not love God and that the two must then go to their different destinies. . . .

Well now in the case of perfect love, if a person loves there is the passion to make the other soul worthy of being loved, for, as I say, this person knows that otherwise he will not continue to love the other. It is a love that costs dearly. This person does everything he can for the other's benefit; he would lose a thousand lives that a little good might come to the other soul. O precious love that imitates the Commander-in-chief of love, Jesus, our Good! (*Way of Perfection*, pp. 64–65)

REFLECTION

When Teresa wrote about other people, she expressed her appreciation for the assistance they provided in the work of the foundations. She also spoke of many other persons with who she communicated for various reasons. Her writings evidence that some people became, and were, her dear friends.

Teresa discerned a difference in her ability to relate with those who also loved God and those who did not. For Teresa, love came to a satisfying fruition only with those who loved God.

As Christians, when we preach the love of God, we proclaim the universal saving grace offered to all people. When we think of our own love in Christ, we would like to think of it as a love that is offered to all people, without discrimination or distinction. To love this way is a continual gospel-based challenge.

Sometimes our love is like mining and refining the good that dwells in another person—indeed the good that *is* the other person. This love actively seeks to foster the good of the other person. At other times, our love quietly recognizes and appreciates the worth of another person. This type of love values the other person for who they are.

In people who are indifferent to the will of God—the source of creation and salvation—we may find obstacles to love, insofar as love is a union of wills. In Teresa's mind, a will guided by God's will and a will without this focus cannot find the union of love. Painful as this may be, an ultimate barrier to a living, reciprocal love exists. Recognizing the limits placed on our ability to love and to be loved by other people is part of the Christian life, too.

❧ Has there been a situation in your life in which you felt obligated to love and yet seemed unable to do so? Does Teresa's understanding of love shed light on this situation? Pray to make a better peace with this situation in your life.

❧ On a piece of paper, make two columns. Title one "To Receive" and the other "To Give." In the first column, write what you want to receive from your Creator. In the second column, write what you wish to give to your Creator. Do the lists balance?

Now envision an important person or situation in your life. Write down what you want to receive from this person or situation. Then write what you want to give this person or situation. Do the columns balance?

❧ Reflect on an event in which someone helped you the way Doña María de Mendoza helped Teresa. How did you show your appreciation for that person? Reflect on an event in which you helped someone in the same fashion. How were you shown appreciation for your help? Praise and thank God for these occasions for expressing love.

❧ Think of someone you find hard to love. Is this person difficult to love because he or she is refusing to be open to the grace of life—in other words, because he or she has no love for God? Consider what this person values and how this person treats God and others. As part of your discernment, dialog with God about this person. If your feelings about this person need healing, ask God for the grace of a forgiving resolution and a hope in regard to this relationship.

❧ Have you ever had a spiritual friend like the one described in "Teresa's Words"? If so, contemplate the goodness of the relationship and awaken a new gratitude for it. If not, envision what a spiritual friend might be like for you. Pray to God about this relationship with a spiritual friend, attempting to discern God's will for you.

❧ Sing your favorite hymn reflectively several times. Awaken your love for God and God's love for you. Two traditional favorites are "Amazing Grace" and "How Can I Keep from Singing?"

GOD'S WORD

My dear friends,
let us love one another,
since love is from God
and everyone who loves is a child of God
    and knows God. . . .

My dear friends,
if God loved us so much,
we too should love one another.
No one has ever seen God;
but as long as we love one another
God remains in us
and his love comes to perfection in us.
This is the proof that we remain in him
and he in us,
that he has given us a share his Spirit.
(1 John 4:7, 11-13)

Closing prayer:

One all-possessing love I ask
My God, my soul centered in You,
Making a delightful nest,
A resting place most pleasing.
(Teresa, *Poetry,* p. 380)

MEDITATION FIFTEEN

Good Works

Theme: Good works that flow from the centered source of love endure, benefit many other people, and honor God.

Opening prayer: Your works, O God, are worthy of praise. May my works be praiseworthy too.

ABOUT TERESA

Once while desiring to render some service to our Lord, I was thinking about how little I was able to do for Him and I said to myself: "Why, Lord, do You desire my works?" He answered, "In order to see your will, daughter." (*Spiritual Testimonies*, p. 412)

Teresa considered the new foundations, the major project of her life, to be both the work of God and her own work. In this work, her will and the will of God were joined.

I never would, or did, leave any monastery until it was in fit condition, had a spirit of recollection, and was adapted according to my wishes. In this matter God greatly favors me, for when there was question of work to be done I enjoyed being the first. And as though I were to live in that house for the rest of my life, I sought to obtain everything, even the smallest thing that would contribute to the tranquility suitable for the life, and so it gave me great happiness to see that everything was in good shape. (*Foundations*, p. 194)

The work of setting up the new houses seldom proved simple. Teresa had to manage all of the various details. For example, in describing the establishment of a house for Carmelite friars, Teresa mentioned seeking permission from two ecclesiastical superiors, sending a friar to gather the things needed for the new house, supervising workers who were preparing the house and enclosure, and instructing Fray John of the Cross about the way of life for the discalced Carmelites. She wanted him to

have a clear understanding of everything, whether it concerned mortification or the style of both our community life and the recreation we have together. . . . He was so good that I, at least, could have learned much more from him than he from me. Yet this is not what I did, but I taught him about the lifestyle of the Sisters. (*Foundations*, p. 163)

Pause: Consider the work you are given to do, and ask yourself, Does my work spring from love?

TERESA'S WORDS

I recall now what I have often thought concerning that holy Samaritan woman. . . . How well she must have taken into her heart the words of the Lord, since she left the Lord for the gain and profit of the people of her village. This explains well what I am saying. And in payment for her great charity, she merited to be believed and to see the wonderful good our Lord did in that village.

It seems to me that one of the greatest consolations a person can have on earth must be to see other souls helped through his own efforts. . . . Happy are those to whom the Lord grants these favors. These souls are indeed obligated to serve him. This holy woman, in that divine intoxication, went shouting through the streets. What amazes me is to see how the people believed her—a woman. And she must not have been well-off since she went to draw water. Indeed she was very humble because when the Lord told her faults to her she didn't become offended (as the world does now, for the truth is hard to bear), but she told Him that He must be a prophet. In sum, the people believed her; and a large crowd, on her word alone, went out of the city to meet the Lord.

So I say that much good is done by those who, after speaking with His Majesty for several years, when receiving His gifts and delights, want to serve in laborious ways even though these delights and consolations are thereby hindered. . . . One of these souls does more good with its words and works than do many others whose works carry the dust of our sensuality and some self-interest. (*Meditations on the Song of Songs*, in *The Collected Works of St. Teresa of Ávila*, vol. 2, pp. 258–259)

REFLECTION

Good works flow from faith, hope, and love. Teresa teaches us about the ebb and flow of prayer coupled with the ebb and flow of service. Teresa's profound interior life was matched by her prodigious public work. Teresa felt that the divinity and humanity of Jesus were at work in both dimensions of life. Teresa was both a highly communicative businesswoman and a poetess of loving union with God. Her work at Carmel and her writings bear witness to the qualitative and quantitative service she rendered in and for the church.

The word "work" has several meanings. It can mean "my job." It can mean "my actions" as well as "the fruition of my actions." Work refers to anything we do. Teresa's understanding of work seemed to cover this wide range of meaning. Good works can be done in our jobs and our actions, or they can be the fruit of our actions. In any case, good works play a key role in Christian spirituality, as they did in Teresa's spirituality.

❧ Meditate on your own good works:

What is the quality of the product of my labors?

Do my labors serve the social good?

What is my manner of working? Am I conscientious? Enthusiastic? Somewhat sloppy? Lackluster?

What motivates me to work the way I do? What impact does my work have on other people? Am I present in my work?

Pray for the graces you need to do "good work" in your job and in your actions.

❧ Pray a litany of thanks to God for the ways in which God is working in your life. For instance,

"For helping me resolve that conflict with Bob, I thank you, God, source of all good work."

"For helping me calm that customer and better serve her, I thank you, God, source of all good work."

❧ Go to your favorite part of the city in which in you live and sit and think about all the workers, past and present, who have made that spot what it is. Thank God for their work.

Some other time, go to your favorite church. Sit and think about all the workers, past and present, whose labors have made that church building and its contents. Thank God for their work.

On a third occasion, go to an undeveloped or down-and-out location and imagine what it could be, or should be, in another ten years. Pray to God that good work will be done there.

🙚 Jot down fifteen things that God has given you to do that you feel are work. Prioritize the list according to how much you find God in each task and then according to each task's objective importance. Compare the lists and bring them to your prayer.

🙚 Spend two hours doing work that you love. Be aware that this work serves human beings, including yourself; thus, your work is an honor to God.

🙚 Meditate on the full story of the Samaritan woman at the well in John 4:1-42.

GOD'S WORD

The [Samaritan] woman put down her water jar and hurried back to the town to tell the people, "Come and see a man who has told me everything I have done; could this be the Christ?" This brought people out of the town and they made their way towards him.

Many Samaritans of that town believed in him on the strength of the woman's words of testimony, "He told me everything I have done." So, when the Samaritans came up to him, they begged him to stay with them. He stayed for two days, and many more came to believe on the strength of the words he spoke to them; and they said to the woman, "Now we believe no longer because of what you told us; we have heard him ourselves and we know that he is indeed the Savior of the world." (John 4:28-30, 39-42)

Closing prayer: Gracious God, give me good work to do and the courage and skill to do it. Indeed, may my whole live be a pleasing work in praise of you and for the good of all my sisters and brothers. Amen. Alleluia!

For Further Reading

Peers, E. Allison. *Handbook to the Life and Times of St. Teresa and St. John of the Cross.* London: Burns Oates, 1954.

Teresa of Ávila. *The Collected Works of St. Teresa of Ávila.* Trans. Kieran Kavanaugh, OCD, and Otilio Rodriguez, OCD. Washington, DC: Institute of Carmelite Studies. Vol. 1, *The Book of Her Life, Spiritual Testimonies, Soliloquies,* 1976. Vol. 2, *The Way of Perfection, Meditations on the Song of Songs, The Interior Castle,* 1980. Vol. 3, *The Book of Her Foundations, Minor Works,* 1985.

———. *The Interior Castle.* trans. Kieran Kavanaugh and Otilio Rodriguez. New York: Paulist Press, 1979.

Welch, John, O Carm. *Spiritual Pilgrims: Carl Jung and Teresa of Ávila.* New York: Paulist Press, 1982.

Acknowledgments

All Scripture quotations used in this book are from the New Jerusalem Bible. Copyright © 1985 by Darton, Longman, and Todd, and Doubleday, a division of RandomHouse, Inc. Reprinted by permission of the publishers.

The quotation from *The Long Loneliness: The Autobiography of Dorothy Day* (New York: Harper and Row, Publishers, 1952). Copyright © 1952 by Harper and Row, Publishers. Reprinted by permission of the publisher.

Quotations from *Saint-Watching*, by Phyllis McGinley (New York: The Viking Press, 1969). Copyright © 1969 by Phyllis McGinley.

Quotations from *The Saint Book*, by Mary Reed Newland (New York: Harper and Row, Publishers, 1979). Copyright © 1979 by The Seabury Press.

Quotations from volume 1 of *The Collected Works of St. Teresa of Ávila* (Washington, DC: ICS Publications, 1976). Translation by Kieran Kavanaugh and Otilio Rodriguez. Copyright © 1976 by the Washington Province of Discalced Carmelites, ICS Publications, 2131 Lincoln Road NE, Washington, DC 20002 USA. Used with permission.

Quotations from volume 2 of *The Collected Works of St. Teresa of Ávila* (Washington, DC: ICS Publications, 1980). Translation by Kieran Kavanaugh and Otilio Rodriguez. Copyright © 1980 by the Washington Province of Discalced Carmel-

Also in the Companions for the Journey Series

Praying with Ignatius of Loyola
Jacqueline Syrup Bergan and
Marie Schwan, CSJ
160 pages, 5¼ x 8, softcover
Item# BSMDE3

Praying with Thérèse of Lisieux
Joseph F. Schmidt, FSC
160 pages, 5¼ x 8, softcover
Item# BSMUE3

Praying with Pope John Paul II
Jo Garcia-Cobb and Keith E. Cobb
176 pages, 5¼ x 8, softcover
Item# BSM1E5

Praying with Francis of Assisi
Joseph M. Stoutzenberger
and John D. Bohrer
144 pages, 5¼ x 8, softcover,
Item# BSMOE3

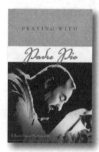

Praying with Padre Pio
Eileen Dunn Bertanzetti
168 pages, 5¼ x 8, softcover,
Item# BSM3E7

Praying with Faustina
Eileen Dunn Bertanzetti
176 pages, 5¼ x 8, softcover,
Item# BSM5E8

To order call 1-800-775-9673 or order online at www.wordamongus.org